Education, Culture and the Emotions

EDUCATION, CULTURE
AND THE EMOTIONS

by

G. H. BANTOCK

INDIANA UNIVERSITY PRESS

Bloomington and London

To
F. R. LEAVIS

Acknowledgments

A number of these essays have been published previously in various journals; and I am indebted to the editors of the following for permission to reprint: *Educational Review, Universities Quarterly, New Society, Education for Teaching, Twentieth Century.* My Inaugural lecture 'The Implications of Literacy' has been previously published by the University of Leicester, and I am grateful to the Publications Board for permission to reprint.

Mr. J. H. Gribble of the Leicester University School of Education kindly read and commented on the essays 'The School and Mental Health' and 'The Education of the Emotions', though I must take full responsibility for what is printed here. I am, as ever, most grateful to my wife for her work in typing and preparing the manuscript and index.

G.H.B.

The University, Leicester

7

Contents

Introduction

'In the beginning all things were in chaos', said Anaxagoras, 'until the mind made order'. And what the mind made, through its power of symbolization, was, of course, a culture, a mode of organizing the various inchoate manifestations of experience in manageable terms. For man had the power to conceive his world, not simply to react towards it, as had the animals. Hence, he built up a number of symbolic modes which enabled him to find a place in the world and to move amongst its multifarious features with a certain degree of confidence. Language afforded him the power to conceptualize and enabled him to assimilate his experience into myth, the discursive arts and sciences; the control over gesture and action introduced ritual and the presentational as well as the practical arts. All such forms are at once expressive and restrictive: they permit raids on the inarticulate, the shapeless, and, at the same time, draw boundaries and erect fences. They involve an amalgam of daring and convention.

It must be obvious that when I speak of 'culture' in this book, I am not speaking of it in that sense of superadded luxury which has attracted the indignation of self-styled plain men since Frederic Harrison found it a 'desirable quality in . . . a professor of belles-lettres'. In my sense, 'culture' forms the inescapable texture of our lives; it provides articulation for our thoughts, our actions and our feelings. It shapes our living. In *Art and Illusion*, for example, Professor Ernst Gombrich has worked out the implications of cultural convention in the specific field of artistic creation. His thesis is that artistic expression develops—

Introduction

in the direction of naturalism, for instance—as the result of an interaction between learned convention and direct perception; and convention tends to dominate. As he puts it: 'Making comes before matching'. There is, he considers, a basic tendency to assimilate any new shape to the patterns an artist has already learned to handle, so that what results stems from the interaction between prior convention and world. 'Painting is an activity', says Professor Gombrich, 'and the artist will therefore tend to see what he paints rather than to paint what he sees'. He needs a vocabulary before he can 'copy' reality; and the nature of the vocabulary will exercise its subtle influence on the way the artist actually conceives the world—a point made also by Wittgenstein in relation to language. To put it in the terminology of Piaget, 'assimilation' takes place and tends to take precedence over 'accommodation'. Even the manifest content of many dreams is determined by local beliefs and culture-patterns. There are, indeed, no percepts without appropriate concepts. Professor Gombrich sums up the situation when he asserts that 'all art originates in the human mind, in our reactions to the world rather than in the visible world itself; and it is precisely because all art is "conceptual" that all representations are recognizable by their style. Without some starting point, some initial schema, we could never get hold of the flux of experience'.[1]

The point here is surely the vital importance of the 'forms' which enable young minds to 'assimilate' experiences and which are built up as a result of their learning experiences. The word 'form' is one that I use a good deal in parts of this book and it is therefore important that I make clear the senses in which I use it. It involves implicitly notions of shape, structure and organization; and, in general, it is related to the 'life' of the culture rather than to the life of the individual. It refers to a set

[1] This is admirably illustrated in the drawings of Balinese children. As their art develops, so they solve their problems of representation by recourse to the ready-made symbolism and design of the 'shadow play', a form of visual entertainment performed in their villages at intervals throughout the year. Cf. J. Belo: 'Balinese Children's Drawings', reprinted in *Childhood in Contemporary Cultures*, ed. by Margaret Mead and Martha Wolfenstein.

of structures, social, emotional and intellectual which an individual inherits from his culture; there are 'forms' of knowledge, 'forms' of behaviour, 'forms' of expression. Even when restructuring takes place, when the individual bursts out of a current form and creates his own, what happens depends enormously on the 'forms' he has inherited. Genius perhaps amounts to the ability to restructure the conventional, to shift the contours into new shapes, to reorder common understanding of experience;[1] but the starting place is always an inherited 'form' which the culture has offered and which the individual has altered as a result of his own accommodations. In so doing, of course, he has created a new structure, a new form—which may or may not be superior to the old one. In science, new structures or 'models' are usually much more fruitful and fertile than the old ones; they represent an advance. Because of the current prestige of science, the tendency is to transfer the value implications of restructuring in that sphere into other areas and assume that the 'new' is necessarily superior, a more dubious proceeding. Or the new may only prove superior to those who have gained social experience as a result of working through the old: there may be a happiness beyond the reach of 'art'—by which is implied current and conventional forms—but such happiness is only obtainable after past 'assimilations' have played their part in the new accommodation.

So the world of our culture is made up of conventions, forms, patterns, models. They all share one general characteristic— they serve both to release human capacities and contain them. Even conventions, which appear to be the most rigid of the four, can help to liberate human powers by demonstrating the limits of the possible and the acceptable. Indeed, they can release in two senses: they offer the opportunity of expression *within* the convention; and, by making known the boundaries of the permissible, they inhibit exhausting hankerings and time-

---

[1] There is a sense however, in which we all adopt the form to our own unique experience, though the modifications are usually slight. Nevertheless we all make *individual* sense as well as *social* sense. Cf. my *Education in an Industrial Society*, pp. 23–24.

Introduction

absorbing aspirations. Yet our age does not happily accept the notion of a limitation. Nearly two centuries of romantic yearnings coupled with a general disintegration of acceptable social forms has taken its toll of many sensible human arrangements; and the notion that a limitation could positively aid expression is foreign to our thinking. Of course, not all limitations do so; but this is a matter of discrimination at the frontiers, not a total rejection of the whole idea of boundaries. What, after all, can inspire the young drug takers of today (and the problem is beginning to assume some alarming proportions) but the desire to escape beyond the demarcations of normal consciousness. And can one really see this as a gain?

The school as a social institution comes within my definition of a form; and its function, too, is both to contain and release. It seeks to release powers of thought and self-expression; but in order to do so, it needs to offer constraints. To this end, it has developed its own rituals and behavioural procedures. Characteristically in our times it is the constraints rather than the opportunities that have come under fire; and, whereas the school has gained in aspiration, it has lost in authority. It is expected to accomplish much more; but its relations with the larger community have become blurred. At once too much and too little is expected of it. For, paradoxically enough, the limitless is always threatened by becoming the most limited. In any form of human activity, dispersal of effort is likely to fail not only in its aims but in the accomplishment which a more confined attempt might have achieved.

The school, indeed, is coming—has come—under a double attack: on its broad conventional aspirations and on its inner guiding principles. Where the former is concerned I intend a reference to what it is thought a formal system can accomplish. Here there is no limit to the pretensions of theorists: practising teachers usually have their feet a little more firmly on the ground. Or have they? I recently attended a conference organized by teachers, at which the boys and girls were asked to consider some of the current social issues in education. What it was thought relevant to discuss is significant. Under the heading

14

of the social implications of education these possibilities were considered:

> Has education so far failed to produce discrimination, understanding and awareness of the full opportunities of life? Ought education to seek to establish particular attitudes and values in society—patriotism, honesty, respect for law and order, morality, racial tolerance, co-operation, duty, responsibility, participation—all are possibilities. Are there others? What of religious and political concepts?

This list in no way exhausts the claims made on the school's attention. Another might well have included the achievement of mental health, for instance. One of the current major needs in education is some attempt to assess just what the day school can reasonably be expected to achieve. My own view is that it must be confined to the induction of young people into certain important areas of understanding, some refined modes of feeling and some reasonably complex practical skills. Certainly, I do not consider that the treatment of the pathological has any place; and this for two reasons. I believe that the rôles of teacher and therapist should be carefully distinguished; and I believe that the introduction of Freudian notions, though necessary where pathological conditions exist, would involve the school at a cruder level of experience than is desirable. My reasons for these beliefs I have set out in the first two chapters; Freudianism, for all its therapeutic benefits has, I believe, coarsened the general texture of our social life because it has encouraged thinking in terms of abnormalities which have no place under general social conditions, apart from pathological states of mind. My point all along is that, to some extent, 'reality' is what we make it; we create the forms of our understanding and thinking, in large measure, through the structures of feeling and apprehension we inherit. Freud has played a part, albeit unwitting, in the current obsession with the morbid and the perverted which informs various of the cultural media of transmission—stage, cinema and television, for example—today. To allow teachers, whose concern is with the normal world and who have neither the benefits of a medical education nor of training analysis, to dabble in the pathological conflicts, conscious or unconscious, of their pupils would seem to me entirely reprehensible.

But this does not betoken a complacency with what does go on in schools. Though these high-level aspirations I have quoted above may go well beyond what the school can reasonably provide, even a more modest assessment of the range of possibilities shows up some deficiencies in modern day schooling. I have written of these elsewhere. Briefly, the curriculum is too intellectualized, especially where the less able are concerned. Indeed, there is a good case to be made out for scrapping the present syllabus for the bottom forty per cent, and concentrating on a curriculum in which a concern for the affective would have pride of place. I have spelt this out at greater length in my *Education in an Industrial Society*: there I promised a fuller consideration of the nature of the education of the emotions at a later date; here, in part, I try to fulfil this promise—in an initial attempt, at least, to remove some of the woolliness from characteristic discussions of the subject. Whether I have succeeded is another matter. But I hope I have provided something discussable.

I also referred above to the attack which was currently being made on the school in relation to what I called 'its inner guiding principles'; and I must now make clearer what I mean. It is possible—though not always very profitable—to discuss the school as a general 'form' which characterises our society; often this leads to the sort of over pretentious claims I have just criticized. But a school, as a complex social institution, can be broken down into a number of subordinate forms relating to specific areas of knowledge, smaller social groupings (some of which are actually referred to as 'forms') and so on, each with their appropriate structures. It is here, among the more progressive educational thinking—and practice—that one notes the introduction of a new fluidity. Concepts of a more rigid nature, in relation to areas of knowledge, such as teaching, instruction, learning, training, give way to concepts which introduce a note of greater flexibility, such as experience,

growth, discovery, experimentation. In considering the procedures relevant to groups of pupils within certain specific
learning areas, the emphasis comes to be not so much on
external structure, whether social or academic, as on internal
involvement. The class is broken up for individual (or small
group) assignments and the logical structure of knowledge
broken down into piecemeal assimilations whose reference
system is made to lie outside the subject structure as such. Or to
sum up the process in another way, the emphasis is placed much
more on the psychological inner than it is on external, formal
coherence. Social and logical 'forms' which traditionally made
their implicit demands dissolve before the more temporary, less
structured manifestations of individual interest and impulse. The
stress rests on the subjective, viewed very much in terms of
spontaneous and often temporary ebullition rather than on
external coherence. The individual has to draw his own boundaries rather than have them 'imposed' on him.

Now this is in line with the general social dissolution of
limits and boundaries, of authorities, of checks and balances in a
variety of spheres. The pervasive cultural climate, as I have
indicated, is 'romantic'; and it is of the essence of romanticism
that it should search for its sanctions 'within' rather than 'without'. Yet, paradoxically, the inner can only strengthen itself by
grappling with healthy and coherent external forms. Even in the
moral sphere, the growing child needs to introject the pro-
hibitions of the adult world as a means to structuring his own
conduct; even if he fights against them, he has something on
which to strengthen his teeth. Furthermore, though the outcome
may be rebellion, he still needs the strength of firm and acceptable rules to afford him security. Obviously, such forms can be
over repressive; but they can also be under sustaining. The en-
couragement of impulse has its place as a safeguard against
petrifaction; but at some stage impulse must be contained for it
to become in any way fruitful and creative.

It is for this reason that the 'education of the emotions' must,
to some extent, be conceived of in terms, not only of expression,
of creative urge, but also of the limits that are implicit in

B   17

Introduction

expression. I have drawn attention, in my essay with this title, to the importance of the particular form taken by such expression; according to the framework within which it is allowed to exist it is emotion disciplined, refined and educated. Articulation in language can alter the development and incidence of an emotion, as Dr. Frederic Wertham shows in *Dark Legend*; there, he explains, by parallels with the stories of Orestes and Hamlet, why a young American Italian came actually to kill his mother. Gino murdered his mother; Hamlet did not. For Hamlet *spoke* daggers to her, Gino used one:

> Hamlet acts with words. That is precisely what Gino could not do. He was consumed by his emotions, centring them more and more on one idea, and never able to give them articulate expression . . . (p. 89)

There were other factors; but the release through virtual rather than actual expression formed a vital factor in transference of the murderous emotion to the symbolic plane.

The lesson extends into more refined spheres. Emotions become manifest, in a variety of guises, internal or external; by learning to disclose themselves in one 'form' rather than another, through one rhythm rather than another, they become different emotions, tamed or more forceful as the case may be. They are more closely allied to cognition than is commonly assumed, for they may be altered by understanding, or, at least, 'informed' with cognitive elements and refined or transformed in the process: a fact which those who advocate too facilely 'hearts not heads in schools' would do well to bear in mind. And this applies to more grandiose and elaborate forms of emotional expression, through myth, for instance. 'Myth', which now implies falsehood, once signified truth. The decay, under rationalist attack, of great mythologies—it happened to the Greeks, and it has happened to us—has left a vacuum which has come to be filled by more fragmentary offerings. Social living, indeed, needs to be sustained by assumptions, longings, aspirations and these betoken the quality of the myths which inform its living. The disappearance of the heroic, whether in the guise of saint or warrior, has necessitated other

Introduction

models for imitation; for the development of identity inevitably involves some assumption of desirable social models, the introjection of an accepted social image. Parents, obviously, supply models; but young people clearly adapt also to social images in the community at large. Recently, posturings disseminated by the mass media have provided attitudes for imitation, as in the case of the young school teacher who lived 'completely under the aegis of a film star'.[1] The need for identification persists in areas where once the great myths performed their pedagogic function. I examine this problem further in 'Myth and the School Child'. Once more, 'forms' of another sort have a part to play. But, today, they can be manufactured to meet the demands of the market, half cynically, as business propositions; and they can, in part, create the tensions they are alleged to alleviate.

The situation has been complicated further by the dissolution of social forms or classes, with their implication of qualitative distinction for the life of society as a whole. With the greater stress on equality we have today, the standards traditionally upheld (in theory, at least) by the superior classes now no longer have any concrete manifestation in the social structure: and thus the notion of quality fails to secure any firm institutionalized manifestation—except perhaps, more peripherally, in the university.

In the emotionally impoverished environment the disappearance of great myth implies, the school, as a culture system, is threatened from two quarters. Its culture is, of course, based on the printed word; and it was the nineteenth century which, faced with the increasing demands of the industrial bureaucratic state, imposed uniquely on a total population the need to learn to read and write. But it forgot to distinguish between the two purposes of literacy. We may need literacy for the purpose of communication; but we tend to assume that communication literacy must also involve culture literacy. I will explain more fully what I mean.

The tight-knit structure of modern industrial society, with its bureaucratic governmental structure and its vast conglomera-

[1] A case quoted in J. P. Mayer: *Sociology of Film*, pp. 153–154.

Introduction

tions of population, needs, for its proper functioning, a literate population for communication purposes; there are a large number of administrative and political tidings, from income tax forms to election messages, which need to be intimated to the people. So the people need to be able to read and write. But, associated with the written and printed word, there is a whole traditional culture of great verbal, emotional, and intellectual complexity, a culture which, in general, was the prerogative of the minority of the highly educated and sophisticated classes; the culture of the people was essentially an oral one and depended on face to face communication, or arose out of the arts and crafts they practised.

It is out of this fact of confusing the literacy of communication with the literacy of culture that many of our present educational difficulties spring. For, of course, the culture of many people today, despite all the schools can do, is not the culture of literacy but the culture of the mass media, of the wide circulation newspaper, of the railway bookstall novel, of the radio, cinema and television. The literacy of communication enables them to indulge in a little light reading; but the literacy of culture is, in general, too intellectually and symbolically complex (whether in words or in scientific formulae) to enable them to encompass it. So we are faced with a conflict of two cultures.

In my Inaugural lecture, 'The Implications of Literacy' I have attempted to analyse the nature of the demands which a book culture makes on those who are being asked to learn to read; at the same time, I have tried to assess some of the changes in psychic awareness which the proliferation of print has made in the Western consciousness. The school makes these demands on a population many of whom are historically ill-prepared to make the effort. The mass media convey their real culture and undermine what the school can offer; and this constitutes the first great threat to what the school stands for. For the media represent a set of values, easier, more immediate in affective appeal, different from the intellectual and emotional refinement implicit in the school at its best. The only solution seems to be to accept the challenge, and by raising the standard of response

20

Introduction

to the media offerings seek to increase the individual's ability to cope with the psychic complexities of good writings.

The second threat arises from the economic and social demands of an industrialized and commercialized society which is thought to need a wide variety of technical competences rather than educated men for its implementation. I have dealt with this problem a good deal in my *Education in an Industrial Society*; but I here reconsider these threats in relation to the university. There are the threats of business, of student culture and of too glib an assumption that disparate modes of intellectual life, modes very necessary to being educated, can be assimilated one to the other. I have considered this last problem in a further consideration of the 'Two Cultures' controversy; for, it should be made clear that forms with different structures must necessarily make different demands on consciousness.

Finally, I have briefly considered the rôle of the teacher, and pointed to the affective element involved in fine teaching, in the impact within the formal structure of the school of personality on personality. And I have wished to pay a brief tribute to one of my own teachers, to whom I have in times past been accustomed to send my manuscripts, T. S. Eliot. I have written about him more comprehensively elsewhere;[1] and I shall shortly be undertaking an even fuller analysis in a small book. But some recognition of the formative power of the great dead, particularly of one who was so intensely aware of

> a lifetime burning in every moment
> And not the lifetime of one man only
> But of old stones that cannot be deciphered;

was imposed, as an act of piety and an act of remembrance. In the immemorial business of bringing up the young we need the historical—indeed, the anthropological—dimension. And it was Eliot's genius to have seen the relevance of time present and time past to time future.

It may seem that some of what I say here contradicts earlier notions I have put forward: that the advocate of individual

[1] In an essay published in *The Educated Man*, ed. P. Nash, A. M. Kazamias and H. J. Perkinson. (John Wiley, New York.)

Introduction

expression has become the apologist for social 'forms'. I do not, myself, see any opposition. Life essentially involves an inter-active process between impulse and constraint, individual élan and the modes of containment implicit in the best social experience. This was the paradox I explored in *Freedom and Authority in Education*. Latterly, in view of the pressure of crude and inadequate social demands, I have urged the importance of individuality: but that individuality should itself in part be the product of a more refined social consciousness. We live poised perpetually in paradox, the juxtapositions that at once give and take away, so that freedom escapes by only a hair's breadth from duress and constraint serves to foster the fuller life. I see these essays as further explorations in a continuing quest.

The School and Mental Health

I

The realization that the healthy development of the affective life is fundamental to the psychic balance of the individual and that a disturbed childhood is the source of much later emotional trouble has led some educationists to urge that the school should deal with much more than the intellectual side of child development. Those who would thus extend the rôle of the school, however, do not completely agree about how the claims of mental health are to be met. At a popular level, Mr. Donald Maclean enjoins that 'schools should be mental hygiene clinics as well as centres of learning', that teachers should be 'trained practitioners of child psychology', and that stability of personality in the child should take precedence over intellectual learning and the acquiring of knowledge. Some theorists seem to be satisfied with what used to be termed attention to the 'whole child'. Others wish to introduce a much more psychoanalytically oriented attitude into the classroom and to make use, in pupil-teacher relationships, of notions derived from depth psychology. The talk here is of the need to cultivate 'insight' in our teachers, to see the functions of pedagogue and of psychiatric social worker as having much in common. I will examine more precisely what the aims and methods of some of these latter advocates of mental health are; and I shall pay particular attention to the work of Dr. W. D. Wall at UNESCO, that of Professor Paul Halmos, of Professor Ben Morris and of speakers at Interprofessional Conferences at

Keele and at Leicester. But it should be made clear at the outset
that there are certain differences between the views of Dr.
Wall, those of Professor Halmos and those of others who also
appeal to depth psychology.

Concern for mental health begins from an extension of what
is already 'progressive' orthodoxy:

> This emphasis upon mental hygiene is a logical extension of
> the trends in modern education, with their increasing emphasis
> upon the development of each child as an individual having his
> own needs and abilities.

Thus writes Dr. Wall, in his Report based upon the work of a
European conference called by UNESCO, which met in Paris
in 1952, *Education and Mental Health*.[1] Impressed by changes in
the structure of the family and in traditions of child-rearing,
Dr. Wall sees the need for a considerable extension of the scope
of the school so that it can provide expert guidance in the
bringing up of children, about which so many parents are unsure of themselves. In a changed environment, where old land-
marks have disappeared,

> The task of forming the character and personality of children
> and adolescents cannot be left to the unaided family and to an
> environment which becomes more and more depersonalised. . . .
> Less and less can the teacher's job be confined to the classroom;
> less and less can the school isolate itself: it must bring family
> and community together for the purpose of educating a new
> generation which . . . may control its own destiny (pp. 271-
> 272).

Though Dr. Wall stresses in this way the need to integrate
the work of home and school, his projected division of labour
stresses the expertise of the teacher. The home supplies emotional conditions of growth of a 'spontaneous' and highly
necessary, but unorganized, kind; the teacher supplies the
expert knowledge to take the place of vanished folk ways in child
rearing. In building up mutual understanding between home

[1] I shall continue to refer to this as the work of Dr. Wall as I have no
means of telling how much of what he writes represents his own views and
how much depends simply on his function as reporter.

and school, the initiative, 'by virtue of his training and his position of responsibility towards a number of children,' will lie with the teacher. And, indeed, as often happens with enthusiasts for new pathways in education, Dr. Wall requires of his teacher a frightening list of attributes. Not only must he be an expert in child development and assist in the proper development of his classes through the application of the latest insights in the psychological field; he is also

> called upon to play the part of applied social scientist. He must constantly challenge his own assumptions and examine his own culture in the light of the present and the future of society. He is called upon to see that the education he gives his pupils exploits the riches and supplements the deficiencies of their environment and brings them to the point at which they may assimilate the changes which are taking place, and play their part in controlling them (p. 272).

It is not surprising that Dr. Wall concludes: 'There is no member of the community with a heavier responsibility' (p. 272).

Dr. Wall, of course, is concerned about the incidence of neurotic anxiety in our civilization and about the necessity of meeting fundamental emotional needs in childhood as a means of guarding against neurosis. Hence the importance of personal relationships in the classroom is stressed—but such is 'progressive' doctrine. Dr. Wall's reference to the unconscious dimension, however, introduces a Freudian element: we are told that 'we must be aware that the constant interaction of teacher and pupil may stimulate more than the intellect, and in a way which subtly eludes normal conscious control' (p. 260). 'Pupils,' it is noted, 'may be used for the teacher's own unconscious ends' (p. 261). Hence suggestions are put forward as to how the teacher training year may be of assistance in aiding the 'maturity' of students; and some examination of these is merited, because they lead us to other psychoanalytically oriented views which seek to assimilate, in some degree, the training of teachers to that of social workers.[1]

[1] Because of the importance of 'unconscious feelings' in the relationship between student and class on teaching practice it has been suggested that

The School and Mental Health

According to Dr. Wall, the students must learn to come to terms with their own unconscious selves, must be convinced of the importance of interpersonal relationships and finally transfer to the classroom situation what they have thus learnt. Training courses must 'challenge unconscious assumptions' and involve the students in a share of responsibility 'until towards the end they plan it largely themselves' (p. 267). Students, then, are to develop as individuals; but group life is important also, since 'socialization and individuation go hand in hand'. Hence the importance of the tutorial discussion group: the 'family set-up' provides a feeling of ' "belonging" ' and so gives a 'sense of security'. The rôle of the tutor becomes assimilated to that of the therapist:

> Sibling problems may be worked out in relation to other students, and parent problems in relation to the tutor. A wise tutor can help an immature student to free himself from parent fixations by playing deliberately whatever form of parental part is required (p. 267).

The techniques of the tutorial group may have to be learnt, and 'the whole staff has to work as a democratic team'. Particularly heavy are the responsibilities of the teacher of psychology: he 'requires something more than an academic knowledge of psychology gleaned from books or a theoretical university course'; the effectiveness of his work 'will depend upon his human qualities'. Sometimes, indeed, he may be called upon to deal with the less severe cases of neurosis, passing on the more serious ones to outside services. Underlying his whole endeavour will be the emergence of an adequate teacher-personality—for 'the development of an adequate personality in all those who will teach children is the first aim of teacher training' (p. 269). Indeed, though it is admitted that 'all teachers ought to be well-educated', we are asked to consider 'whether affective and personal qualities are not more important than a high level of

---

new methods of school practice supervision based on the social 'casework model' should be adopted. Cf.: 'A New Approach to Supervision of Teaching Practice' by I. Caspari and S. J. Eggleston (*Education for Teaching*, November, 1965).

The School and Mental Health

intelligence for many teachers, for example, those who teach children of pre-school age or in the early primary years'.

The implications of the above are that students are beset with 'problems' which the training course needs to solve, and that the schools need emotionally balanced personalities rather than intellectually capable people. Why there should be thought to be some opposition between the two qualities is not made clear. What is specifically interesting about these recommendations, however, is the part played by concepts developed in depth psychology. Professor Paul Halmos, for instance, urges the 'understanding of man' as the central purpose of courses in education and social work (I, p. 22).[1] Fundamental to this understanding is an 'understanding in depth'; for, he explains,

> Rules, such as 'frustration tends to lead to aggression' or 'too much permissiveness is anxiety-producing' are propositions which simply cannot be understood without an empathic and rapport-like identification with one who is being frustrated and reacts with aggression or with one who is anxious because he doesn't know what to do with too much freedom and tolerance (I, p. 23).

In the production of this empathic state, we must reactivate in the student replicas of the emotional difficulties he is likely to meet: 'A psychological sensitization may mean that the student is called upon to reopen a closed chapter of his emotional history' (p. 24). Only thus, presumably, can full 'insight' be obtained. At any rate, Professor Halmos accepts that 'teaching personality is an interference with the personality development of the student'. But teachers and social workers should be taught the same theory of personality development which 'must be pivoted on the psycho-analytic theory for no other theory of human motivation available today can offer us explanatory hypotheses of equal scope, depth and predictive power' (I, p. 27), though he notes some reservations in accepting the whole range of psychoanalytic theory.

[1] The reference is to *The Sociological Review Monograph* No. 1: Papers on the Teaching of Personality Development. July 1958. (Published at Keele). There are three of these Monographs which report successive conferences held on Personality Development in the training of teachers and social workers.

The School and Mental Health

Professor Halmos is not an isolated instance of those who are willing seriously to disturb students emotionally as a means of making them aware of personality factors. He even urges, against those psychoanalytic professionals who would advise the eschewing of depth psychology except where proper therapeutic training has been received, that any neglect of possibilities would be *morally* indefensible. For he recognizes that: '*All the technical issues I have raised demand moral decisions*' (II, p. 145).[1] A moral ideal is certainly in the mind of Professor Ben Morris, too, in making somewhat similar recommendations concerning the training of teachers.[2] Professor Morris has stated that the 'central psychological concept in modern discussion of mental health' is the 'concept of unconscious mental process' (p. 47) on the grounds that 'experience is emotional', that 'mental health is largely a matter of the emotions' (p. 46). Hence it is not surprising to find him criticizing current training in this way:

> . . . our present practice of ensuring a good general academic standard, a mastery of one or two subjects, a bookish knowledge of academic educational and psychological theory and the acquisition of some tricks of the trade is woefully inadequate (p. 97).

At the moment, as a result of the 'present conduct of our whole educational system', the 'majority of students' are still 'very immature persons at the beginning of their course. They are generally well-equipped with examination knowledge and as a consequence severely verbally biased'. Hence their need for exposure to the realities of the classroom, in turn the focus of 'continuous tutorial discussions':

> Such discussions in small groups should aim at being quasi-therapeutic ones, where the real problems of teaching and of interpersonal relations in school and college can be studied in the light of personal experience (p. 99).

Though Professor Morris does very explicitly warn against turning teachers into 'amateur psychologists and psychiatrists'

[1] *The Sociological Review Monograph* No. 2 ed. P. Halmos, Sept. 1959.
[2] In *Studies in Education* No. 7: The Bearings of Recent Advances in Psychology in Educational Problems (Evans Bros., University of London Institute of Education) 'Mental Health in the Classroom'.

or trying to teach 'a great deal about unconscious psychodynamics to the *majority* of students', nevertheless, the make-up and implications of his quasi-therapeutic groups are interesting. His recommended technique is derived from Bion's experiments in discussion with neurotic patients. Though we are assured that such work as is undertaken 'is not remotely the equivalent of a psychoanalysis', yet it still 'required the guidance of someone with special skill'. The nature of the skill is not made very clear in a subsequent footnote, except that these group 'leaders' will be trained by a qualified psychoanalyst or the 'analyzed person who has made a special practical study of groups'. Again, these people are to be capable of 'guiding quasi-therapeutic group discussions among teachers and other professional groups' (p. 106). The general aim seems to be to enable us to come to 'passable terms with our unconscious selves'. Professor Morris, indeed, looks forward to the time when every training department

> has on its staff one psychologist who has had a personal analysis. It would be the duty of such a person to teach about the unconscious aspects of motivation and to provide appropriate group experience for those advanced students in the area who were preparing themselves for positions of responsibility in the training of teachers (p. 108).

In this way, teachers will be able to come to terms with the child in themselves, as a preliminary to that 'adventure in mutuality' in which Professor Morris sees the nature of education.

The psycho-therapeutic orientation, then, seems reasonably clear; some of the advocates of mental health in the school would wish to blur, to a quite marked degree, the distinction between teacher and therapist: as Dr. Halmos says:

> . . . whilst one should maintain a careful and critical attitude in the face of suggestions that teaching and therapy are in fact complementary aspects of education . . . one should also vigorously support research and experiment aimed at devising techniques in which teaching and therapy may be combined.[1]

---

[1] Cf. *The Sociological Review Monograph*, No. 2.

Furthermore, by means of a rather bogus semantic analysis of the two terms, he brings them into a close relationship, urging that 'in a very important sense the separation of the concepts of "teaching" and "therapy" is an arbitrary one'. After pointing to uses of the word 'teach' in contexts associated with healing (e.g. 'the polio victim who is *taught* to walk again') Professor Halmos concludes:

> We must now revise our resistance to experimentation in hybrid techniques to deal with the all-too-frequently hybrid problems of life (II, pp. 130–131).

II

There are, so far as I can see, two major reasons for the attempt to assimilate a quasi-therapeutic function to that of teaching. 'Insight' (by which is meant awareness based on Freudian understanding) is essential for teachers because of the incidence of neurosis in our modern communities and

> prevention . . . is well-nigh impossible without adding to the insight of those in particular who are in charge of children. (*Towards a Measure of Man* by P. Halmos, p. 177.)

Furthermore, it is argued that a purely intellectual discussion of Freudian notions is inadequate for training purposes; some direct participation leading to affective awareness in group situations appears to be a minimum requirement for effective teacher understanding. Professor Morris, as we have seen, talks about 'quasi-therapeutic group discussions'; Professor Halmos goes further and accepts the possibility that the students may have to reopen past affects. Both, indeed, accept the notion that the student may suffer considerable disturbance in the process of insight gaining.[1]

I would agree that teachers should be made aware of the possibility of neurosis, springing from affective sources, in their pupils. I would wish to quarrel on moral grounds with advocates

[1] Both, however, rely simply on rational persuasion through books and articles to persuade us to take the steps towards insight-giving that they favour. They cannot, therefore, think that intellectual persuasion is quite useless!

of this line of action, however, because of the procedures they consider necessary to bring such awareness about. I quarrel, that is, with the notion that the teacher should himself in any respect be expected to fulfil a therapeutic rôle,[1] or that he should be expected to have any more understanding than is necessary for anything but the very first step in diagnosis.

At first sight, superficially, perhaps, there would appear to be a certain overlapping of rôles between the teacher and the therapist. At the very least the aims of both seem to be partly moral, and rationalistic. A crucial point arises from the admitted affective influence on intellectual life, an influence which, as we shall see, Freud has emphasized. The teacher, it is plausibly argued, cannot, in any case, now confine his rôle simply to that of 'teaching' in the way in which the rôle was traditionally conceived. The forces of affective life, hidden in the id, manifesting themselves as unconscious motivations, may not only interrupt the children's powers of learning and concentration; they may even influence the teacher himself in ways of which (naturally) he is not aware. As Freud, addressing the ego, puts it:

> In all cases . . . the news that reaches your consciousness is incomplete and often not to be relied on. . . . Even if you are not ill, who can tell all that is stirring in your mind of which you know nothing or are falsely informed. (*Collected Papers*, Vol. IV, p. 355.)

Hence the claim, as we have noted, that teaching is 'in some respects necessarily a therapeutic relationship'.

I believe, however, that a great deal of confusion is introduced into the situation by the use of the word 'therapy' in any of its forms. For when we talk about the need for therapy, we imply the treatment by some means, usually medical, of a pathological condition; the notion of 'disease' seems to be inseparable from it. The implication is of some morbid state which necessitates the application of specialized techniques in order to return the patient to 'normal'. In other words, there are two important factors in any situation demanding the application of

[1] In the technical, Freudian sense of the term.

therapeutic methods: one, the need to posit an initially diseased state, and the other the application of specialized techniques, having in mind simply the reform of the diseased state. It is *possible* that some at least of the people who employ the term may be using it metaphorically—in the way in which modern philosophers use it when they refer to their job of linguistic analysis as fulfilling a 'therapeutic' aim. If this is so, it should be made clear; but among the educationists whose work we have examined it is certainly not so employed. I think this is clear from my analysis of their views.

Now the upholder of the therapeutic importance of the teacher's function often argues—and he will be able to draw sustenance from Freud's own frequently repeated assessment of the situation—that, in fact, we are none of us completely normal; that, to some extent, we are all subject to abnormalities which may affect us in varying degrees at varying times. Freud himself puts it:

> For the borderline between normal and what are called morbid mental states is to some extent a purely conventional one; furthermore it is so fluid that probably everyone of us oversteps it many times in the course of a day. (Quoted by Ernest Jones: *Life of Sigmund Freud*, Vol. 3, p. 449.)

Indeed, such a view is accepted by Dr. Halmos when he asserts that

> The beginning of effective insight-giving is to demonstrate to our students that there are not two psychologies, that is a normal and abnormal psychology, and that a continued insistence on this division blocks the way to understanding man (I, p. 26).

What interests me about Freud's account is the way in which it assumes the possibility of making sensible statements about something as abstract and hypothetical as another's 'state of mind'. For indeed, the only way in which we can come to any understanding of what is going on in another's mind is through his *actions*, through what he does or through what he says. Only by watching him and interpreting what he does and says can we arrive at any conclusions—which even then need to be interpreted with care—concerning what is going on in his mind. And it is only when in some way or other he behaves in a manner which, by the standards of social convention and acceptable behaviour in our society, would seem to be distinctly odd that we have any right to suggest that there is anything abnormal about him. Freud's statement about normality and abnormality then, can only be interpreted either as a suggestion that, if we watch people, we will notice behavioural oddities much more frequently than we would if we had not been warned, or as a piece of autobiography.

Unless, then, people tell us about odd feelings or desires or unless we observe indications—they may, of course, be slight and subtle ones—of unusual or queer behaviour, it seems to me that we have no right whatsoever to assume irrationality or some form of abnormality. We only need to seek explanations of behaviour—except for some specialized purpose, like a psychological enquiry—when that behaviour strikes us as peculiar; and, even then, there may be perfectly simple explanations, necessitating no deeper search; for some at least of the oddities we encounter.

Now the notion of therapy, as a constant part of the teacher's job, assumes the continuing presence of the abnormal or diseased or morbid. Yet when we look further into those statements of Freud which, if I am right, have led people to make such an assumption we find, in fact, that apart from the explicit statements or actions of others, we have no evidence whatsoever to justify any such assumption. The only possible reasonable mode of behaviour for a teacher, then, is to act as if the children in front of him demonstrated those characteristics which we have come to expect of 'normal' children of the age concerned, and only to adapt his procedures radically if he encounters something strange in relation to expectations.

Let us assume for the moment, however, that he *has* encountered something which makes him suspect that all is not as it seems to be. What is he to do? To some extent, of course, it will depend on the degree of oddity, and the inability to satisfy himself as to possible reasonable or conventional explanations.

But if this situation arises, what is to be done? An entirely different set of procedures become relevant. Here the morbid, diseased state had arisen, and the procedures necessary for treatment, cure, healing become necessary.

Now there are a variety of reasons why it is undesirable for one person to operate in the two different rôles with the same child. It is in any case not very likely that one and the same person will be adequately trained in the exercise of the two techniques, teaching and therapy, though, of course, it is not in any way impossible. But the relationships between child and therapist and child and teacher are of quite a different order. Teachers and therapists are concerned about different things: the teacher seeks to work with the child's interest in the real world, interpreted as either the external phenomena of sense experience or the internal one of conscious wishes and desires provided these betray neither unusual nor pathological symptoms. The therapist concerns himself only when the external or internal worlds appear under pathological aspects, when the aim is the understanding of what lies behind the symptoms, not the conscious manipulation of the external world in the name of curiosity and creativity. Susan Isaacs, who fully understood the distinction, says:

> . . . the unconscious wishes as such are not, and cannot be within (the teacher's) competence—any more than the teaching and training of the child in skilful manipulation or understanding of the *external* world is within the competence of the analyst. (*Social Development*)

In the pursuit of their respective rôles, it can also be noted that the analyst employs a degree of impersonality in relationship with the child which is no necessary part of the teacher's rôle. And Susan Isaacs adds the warning: 'The explosive material of the unconscious can only safely be handled by trained analysts working in a proper technically controlled analytic environment.'

I cannot, then, think that the teacher is at any time called upon to fulfil a rôle in any way analogous to that of the therapist; and I believe that the teacher situation can only be confused by failing to preserve the necessary boundaries. I believe, too, that such confusion may lead to an over-valuation of certain attitudes on the part of the teacher, particularly one of what is called 'permissiveness'; and I would suggest that, in the face of what many have pointed to as the creative force of tension in the teaching situation, the emphasis on permissiveness may perhaps spring in part from a confusion between the necessity of permissiveness in the analytic situation referred to above and its desirability in the teaching. I would suggest, too, that the desire to avoid tension in the classroom may have been influenced by Freud's model of the release from excitation followed by a state of equilibrium in accordance with the law of constancy as the desirable human norm. (There are probably other, socio-political democratic, egalitarian factors involved also—a pervasive anti-authoritarianism.) Indeed, I often suspect that the imputation of unconscious motivations springs from a concern to urge the virtues of a certain sort of teacher personality, the implication being that those who depart from this idea pattern must be in the grip of unconscious anxieties etc. which make them 'authoritarian'. The imputation of unconscious influences on behaviour can all too easily be used as an explanation of personality traits of which we disapprove. It might be as well to bear in mind that there are 'permissive' personalities whose unwillingness to make up their minds or to take decisions would in itself seem to be neurotically motivated—it results, that is to say, in distinctly odd behaviour.[1]

I have been suggesting, so far, then, that those who like Freud himself on at least one occasion, would urge that 'every ... person (concerned with the bringing-up of children) should receive a psychoanalytic training, since without it children ... must remain an inaccessible problem to him', have no grounds for their contention. A therapeutic situation would, of course, demand such a training; a normal teaching or parental one does not.

There are, of course, further possible objections. I have al-

[1] Especially as, on closer acquaintance, they often reveal quite strong authoritarian leanings under the permissive façade. This feature, indeed, will be found in the great classic progressives like Rousseau. Other oddities can include denial of legitimate responsibilities and withdrawal of contact.

The School and Mental Health

ready drawn attention to the quite absurd load of qualifications and qualities which the modern teacher is expected to have. To expect him to acquire even more skills—and those of a highly ambiguous and difficult nature—and to run the risk, in the process of acquiring them, of serious emotional disturbance, seems to me to partake both of the impractical and the unethical. That teachers are likely to become genuinely competent in this field in the space of time available is unlikely, and whatever competence accrues is likely to be more than offset by the moral licence afforded to probe into the lives of their pupils in the possibility of discovering affective disorders. One recognizes indeed the force of Virginia Woolf's antipathy, quoted so tellingly by Lady Wootton, to 'the peculiar repulsiveness of those who dabble their fingers self approvingly in the stuff of others' souls.' The ends suggested—harmony and balance, or optimum disbalance leading to rational progress[1]—seem at first sight so admirable, so reasonable in a world where there is always so much pain, that one's repugnance at the therapeutic (quasi) groups seems an element of personal fastidiousness one ought to put aside in the name of the general good. It is only when one realizes—in relation to recalcitrant human nature as it is—the possibilities opened up by this sort of thing that one's repugnance comes to have a greater validity. Nor is there any guarantee that the would-be teacher would be convinced by participation in quasi-theraputic groups of any need for change. Where there is neurosis, the individual has a strong motive for undergoing the emotional pain—for that is what it is—of cure. But there is no reason to assume that the average teacher, even if he achieves some 'insight', is likely to be convinced that any reorientation of his own personality is necessary, for he may, quite legitimately, have a different set of moral ideals from those implicit in the practise of therapy. (That Freudian therapy has a moral ideal is implicit in Professor Morris's statements and in Freud himself.)[2] At least a possible result of such psychothera-

[1] It is interesting to note that advocates of mental health often do not agree as to what constitutes the healthy person.
[2] Cf. 'Freud and Education' pp. 44-64

peutic groups is that the sceptical will be unconvinced, the unscrupulous further armed, and the conscientious more anxious. For behind all this emphasis on the acquiring of insight lies the rationalist assumption that if only the world knew its own mind a little better, it would automatically prefer the good to the bad—'insight' is supposed to lead to morally superior behaviour. Advocates of this point of view forget, for instance, the action of the 'hidden persuaders', those who attempt to make a good commercial proposition out of insights gained from a knowledge of depth psychology.

There is also, of course, the problem of the extent to which one would have a moral right to practise techniques which might lead, in Professor Morris's words, to the development of 'quite serious symptoms of personal maladjustment.' This is particularly so among people—those who come to be trained as teachers—who do not come expecting any form of therapeutic treatment, quasi or otherwise. The notion that such treatment should become an obligatory part of a training course—which is presumably what would happen if some of these advocates had their way—would lay those who supported such notions open precisely to the sort of criticism that Lady Wootton has so cogently urged against the activities of psychiatric social workers in her *Social Science and Social Pathology*. As I believe these to be very relevant to the case of the intending teacher who comes expecting the solution to one sort of problem—how shall I best convey a given body of academic or practical material to a class of children—and is, willy-nilly, involved in the working out of another, the need for any solution to which he may never become rationally convinced of, I shall examine Lady Wootton's arguments at some length. For the intending teacher would be very much in the position of the caseworker's client.

Lady Wootton refers to ideas about the rôle of the social caseworker which appear to involve 'claims to powers which verge upon omniscience and omnipotence'. The approach she criticizes is one which involves penetration 'below what is called the "presenting problem" to the "something deeper" that is supposed to be underneath.' She not only shows some scepticism about the reality of the 'something deeper,' on the grounds that it necessitates the claim to 'understand other people better than they understand themselves,'[1] she also remarks tartly that 'The suggestion that complex problems of personal unhappiness . . . can be resolved by a young woman with an academic training in social work is difficult to take seriously.' Her suggestion is, indeed, that the search for deeper problems may distract attention from the very real emergencies which drive people to seek help and that, in effect, claims to work at this deeper level demonstrate a 'lamentable arrogance'.

The accusation of 'arrogance' leads us to consider the nature of Lady Wootton's moral repugnance for certain recommended procedures in social casework. Informing her distaste can be detected her endorsement of a specific historical conception of human personality, one which involves a claim to personal privacy matched by an acceptance of personal responsibility for actions performed; it is a view which may be summed up as liberal, rational and protestant. People, Lady Wootton argues, should be accepted as morally responsible agents who by and large mean what they say and have the right to be treated as if they did. Implicitly she speaks as a supporter of a liberal, democratic society: for example, in contrasting the rather more modest claims of the 'functionalist' school of social workers with those of the 'organismic,' she shows some sympathy with the former on the grounds that the 'arrogant readiness of their rivals to manage other people's lives does violence to the fundamental principles of a democratic society.' She recognizes that people who request assistance may have problems in their lives other than the ostensible one; but this is not, in her opinion, 'to admit that those who are invited to deal with one matter are entitled to explore others, or that it is proper to give professional training in the art of extracting from those who seek help on one problem details of others of a more intimate, personal nature.'

[1] A rather doubtful argument: there are clearly occasions when observers can understand things about people which they don't understand about themselves.

The School and Mental Health

Nor ought students who come expecting to learn how to teach be expected to have their emotional life tampered with through the employment of techniques they do not even understand.

I believe that this argument based on the right, in a still liberal society, to be accepted as a moral agent with a corresponding right to certain privacies, deserves very serious consideration. In fact it is relevant in a considerable range of instances where work in the social sciences (of which, for certain purposes, education can be considered one) is being undertaken, as Professor Edward Shils has shown in an admirable essay entitled 'Social Inquiry and the Autonomy of the Individual'.[1] There he indicates some of the main ethical problems raised by the scientific study of man's behaviour. These arise, he says:

> from the confrontation of autonomy and privacy by a free intellectual curiosity, enriched by a modern awareness of the depth and complexity of the forces that work in us and implemented by the devices of a passionate effort to transform this awareness into scientific knowledge.

It is clear that these quasi-therapeutic groups cannot function, without resorting, in some measure, to a sort of probing which to many people is morally repugnant, involving, as it does, the revelation of intimacies most people prefer to hide— on grounds which, so far as I can see, are perfectly defensible. Again, to think that in a nine months' training course it is possible to bring about considerable alteration in personality— for that is basically the aim of personality development courses —in addition to all the other things a course must do, is really so much pretentious nonsense. The only sort of alteration it is morally defensible to envisage is that which comes from the rational persuasions of such a course, for which evidence should be duly produced. In the process of learning how to teach, a certain amount of information about how children learn, what can be expected from children with certain socio-economic backgrounds—and so on, is made available to the student. If he assimilates this information, his attitude to the job is likely to undergo a certain amount of development—though whether

[1] Reprinted in *The Human Meaning of the Social Sciences*, ed. D. Lerner.

this could really amount to something warrenting the description 'change of personality' is probably a conceptual point of some difficulty. Nevertheless, these are the right and proper changes to induce in an education course in a university. There is no excuse for placing intending teachers in a situation where the intention is that their personalities should be affected by means of which they have no prior knowledge. There is not even the excuse that they have come seeking 'help', in any sense of the word which would explain some degree of therapeutic orientation.

There is, however, a further important point to be raised. Already, in my exposition, there have been hints concerning the anti-intellectual element in the mental health movement. Dr. Wall, though concerned about learning to some extent, considers:

> Where the staff of a school consider it to be their sole duty to dispense an intellectual culture, to enforce a verbal learning and to hold aloof from the personal lives of their pupils, it is likely that serious and lasting damage is being done to a considerable number of the pupils. Much could be done by the schools themselves, without abandoning traditional values and standards, to mitigate their impact. (*Education and Mental Health*, p. 173.)

Learning, he points out, is a 'process with emotional, maturational and intellectual aspects' (p. 29). Certainly, he considers 'the development of a sound work attitude' is one of the 'major mental health as well as educational goals of the primary school' (p. 89). There are, however, other more extreme expressions of anti-intellectualism urged at the Interprofessional Conferences. In the development of insight, as I have noted, there are warnings against thinking that 'an intellectual grasp of psychological processes is insight'. For, it is said, 'one of the most subtle defences against feeling is the flight into intellectualization' (II, p. 30). Mrs. Winnicott, indeed, warns against the student social worker with a high I.Q.: 'In some, the high intelligence can have been exploited to the cost of the rest of the personality' (II, p. 32). Dr. Halmos states:

... in our educational value-system we seem to devote most of our attention to a boy getting a distinction in French or Physics in the G.C.E.O. whilst we may breezily assure ourselves that it is not really our business to help this boy stop having nightmares every night. It is remarkable how we maintain an outmoded educational ideology in the face of compelling facts (I, p. 32).

Professor Roger Wilson, who is certainly not an extremist and who has some sensible things to say about the need to keep teaching and social work separate, urges that

It becomes of less comparative importance to transmit the minor and limited disciplines of reading, writing, arithmetic and obedience to authority as it becomes more important to help people to choose responsibly within a complex and changing society whose patterns are, in some respects, very fluid (I, p. 121).

Furthermore, Professor Tibble believes that

... a preoccupation with subject-matter and content tends to blind the teacher to the deeper aspects of the task ... our task as trainers is to help him to displace this preoccupation with subject-matter from the forefront of his consciousness to the background so that he is free to concentrate on the reaction of his pupils as individuals, on the learning process as distinct from the end-products of it. (II, p. 51.)

How the process can be considered apart from the ends the process is supposed to serve is not explained; furthermore, the reactions of pupils must take place in a context, and subject-matter will be relevant to that context. Such statements are in line with the same speaker's view that 'teaching would gain if it were more commonly thought about as a kind of social work' (II, p. 53). Again, Mrs. Kellmer Pringle quotes with approval from Professor P. E. Vernon:

'Though we still tend, perhaps, to think that the main aim of schooling is to impart information and train children's intellects, the real crux of the teacher's job (except possibly at advanced grammar school and university levels), which makes such great demands on his or her emotional energy, is the establishment of personal relationships and the control of children's delinquent and other unacceptable behaviour, particularly when classes are large.' (II, 110–111.)

The School and Mental Health

But the particular nature of the personal relationship and the terms of the discipline exercised must inevitably be controlled by the 'form' of the typical commerce between teacher and taught—and this commerce is essentially a pedagogic one. Relationships don't exist in a vacuum, they are structured by the contexts in which they occur.

The implied split between the emotional and the intellectual life of the individual is in line with the Freudian view which stresses the importance of the often unconscious affective elements in the personality and tends, despite Freud's own fundamentally rationalist position, to suspect reason as the creator of rationalizations. This constitutes progressive orthodoxy, also, which has always tended to emphasize 'hearts' rather than 'heads' in school. The over-glib employment of the division tends to ignore the fact that there is not a wide range of behaviour which is the result of either emotional or intellectual factors to the exclusion of the other; most of our conscious actions are likely to involve some measure of combination of the two.

But the insistence on the primacy of emotional factors permits the excuse of 'emotional immaturity' to be used to 'explain' various types of anti-social behaviour, with a consequent diminution of that sense of personal responsibility which the intellectualist tradition imposed. Paradoxically, the effect which a predominantly rationalist ethic (the Freudian) has had in popular estimation has been to throw doubt on the very efficacy of the intellect itself. In school the danger manifests itself in covert attacks on the importance of academic learning in the only sort of institution which our society devotes to this purpose. That I myself am not entirely happy about the range of the traditional curriculum in no way leads me either to underestimate the importance of what is now done for the future welfare of our able children, nor to ignore the part played by the intelligence in such attention to the affective life I wish to promote through the extended curriculum I have in mind. It is only with our disturbed children (recognized as such by their behaviour) that the resources of depth psychology need to be brought into play; the rest can be helped by the realization that the scope of understanding the school needs to undertake extends much wider than to the intellect narrowly concerned and yet remains within the bounds of the normal skills and human satisfactions men have traditionally sought and acquired; and that in emotional education the intellect plays some part.[1]

Of course, I appreciate that by the converted—and in speaking in this context one tends to fall into a vocabulary with evangelical overtones—my criticisms will be dismissed as simply indicative of my own unconscious resistance. May be, of course: no man, by definition, can know his own unconscious. But I have produced *arguments* which have a life beyond that of their author. These arguments need answering; until they have been answered the case for therapy in schools must remain under a cloud.

[1] Cf. 'The Education of the Emotions', pp. 65–86.

2

Freud and Education

In this paper, I shall be particularly concerned with implications of Freud's views on the nature of the child and of his conception of 'reality', and I shall want to refer briefly to the relevance of these views to educational practice. At the same time, it should be realized that Freud himself made few overt comments on education and his notions about childhood were in the main theoretically formulated in order to explain certain phenomena noted in the history, reconstructed during the analytic session, of adult patients. They were not derived from much first-hand experience of child therapy or from experimental observation of child behaviour. Childhood, then, to Freud, is a theoretical construct, formulated to 'explain' adult behaviour and based on adult memories. Nevertheless the observations of subsequent child therapists would seem to have confirmed a good deal of what Freud thus reconstructed; at least, the construct would appear to be clinically applicable.

Although psychology and philosophy, formerly not differentiated in the writings of philosophers, split asunder, and psychology, in the nineteenth century, acquired the tentative status of a separate discipline, it has nevertheless remained clear that a psychology rests ultimately on an ontology, a metaphysic of man. Freud, indeed, implicitly recognizes this by calling *his* psychology a 'meta-psychology', thus implying a speculative as well as an empirical element.

For Freud, man was an animal, and nothing more than an

44

animal. Such a view was based partly on empirical grounds, partly on metaphysical. His early researches in the field of neurology led him to conclude that the nervous system of the higher animals did not contain elements different *in kind* from those of the lower animals, but only different in degree. He was influenced in his early days by Darwinian evolutionary views; and he later attempted to demonstrate the evolutionary pattern in the development of the ego out of the 'impersonal primordial group of impulses he designated as the Id', as Ernest Jones puts it. The metaphysical implications of his theory of man emerge in his denial of any religious or supernatural element in man's development: 'The development of man up to now', he asserted in *Beyond the Pleasure Principle*, 'does not seem to me to need any explanation differing from that of animal development.' Hence, as Ernest Jones says, 'The world of nature seemed all-embracing and he could find no evidence of anything outside it.'

This conception of man was further reinforced by an influence especially noticeable in the first tentative exposition of his meta-psychological views in the *Project* of 1895. Here, as James Strachey pointed out, he seems to have derived much from Helmholtz's school of physiology, according to which neuro-physiology and consequently psychology were governed exclusively by chemico-physical laws. The law of constancy was the fundamental principle—a mechanistic one—in terms of which Freud conceived the working of the whole psychic apparatus; according to this the nervous system strove to keep the pitch of excitation to which it was subjected at a constant level.

A consequence of considering the child exclusively a product of the natural world is that this development comes to be regarded as subject to universally valid scientific laws. Psychic growth, as well as physical, follows a universal pattern, and all men must pass 'successfully' (whatever that implies) through a series of well-defined stages in order that they shall achieve maturity or 'normality'. Particularly is this so in libidinal development, when the individual moves through a series of stages prescribed by heredity. There are, according to Freud, two broad phases of sexual development—that covering the first five or six years and that stemming from puberty—divided by the 'latency period'. Infantile sexuality manifests itself in the activity of a whole number of component instincts, dependent upon the erotogenic zones of the body. Thus psychic development for Freud, as Ernest Jones puts it in his biography, involves

> . . . a ceaseless search for the endless possible ways in which various fundamental biological drives may achieve satisfaction; and the complicated 'reaction-formations' that serve as defences against the ever present dread of these drives in their primitive form.

Freud's theories of instincts (he changed his views) involve a fundamental rejection of that optimistic tradition concerning man's moral nature stemming from the eighteenth century Enlightenment. His hypotheses concerning the sexual and aggressive destructive instincts led him to two very important formulations. The assumption of natural goodness was dismissed as one of those 'unfortunate illusions' which 'bring only disaster'. Freud, indeed, would have no truck with the notion of human being as 'gentle friendly creatures wishing for love': '*Homo homini lupus*' much more adequately sums up his assessment of the situation. Nor does he regard children as 'pure and innocent', except in the sense that their youth renders it necessary to consider them as amoral. Until contact with reality necessitates 'reaction formations' of instinctual strivings, children comprise simply bundles of egocentric, satisfaction-seeking impulses; they 'assert their animal nature naïvely enough and demonstrate persistently that they have yet to learn their purity'.

The other feature of Freud's pessimistic assessment of human development involves the stress he laid on the emotional, passional life, in the sense that stability of the rational conscious ego or intellective side was constantly threatened by the irrational, unconscious id, and lived a life of precarious balance. Thus the whole optimism of the rationalistic tradition of the Enlightenment, which looked to the gradual elimination of the 'evil' in man's nature through the spread of reason, was called into question:

Freud and Education

Psychoanalysis unhesitatingly ascribes the primacy in mental life to affective processes, and it reveals an unexpected amount of affective disturbance and blinding of the intellect in normal no less than in sick people. (*The Claims of Psycho-analysis to Scientific Interest*)

In so far as Freud's therapeutic purpose is resolutely rationalistic, he certainly cannot be termed an irrationalist. Yet his view of the 'natural man' is quite different from that, say, of Rousseau. Rouseau assumed that the inherent drive, in childhood, towards self survival (' amour de soi-même'), if carefully watched lest 'need' degenerate into 'caprice' and 'amour de soi-même' become 'amour propre', was essentially 'good', and moral in the sense that its indulgence would not lead beyond the harmonization of all with each.

In contradistinction to this view of the Enlightenment, Freud posited the egocentric, instinctual strivings of the primitive being. His 'state of nature' is Hobbesian rather than physiocratic. And yet, 'progressive' thinking in education, so profoundly influenced by notions of natural goodness and theories of free inner development untrammelled by obtrusive adult or pedagogic influence, assimilates without difficulty so sombrely based a theory of human development. How this comes about can only be made clear from an analysis of that triad of forces, through the operation of which, in the Freudian scheme, the 'natural' becomes 'civilized' or 'socialized'. I refer to the id, the ego and the super-ego.

The id is the seat of the instincts and passions, totally lacking in organization or moral sense. Its essential characteristic is that of being 'foreign to the ego', though it is from the id that the ego gradually differentiates out. The uninhibited indulgence of the id's instinctual strivings would make of social life an impossibility; there are two restraining factors, aspects of the developing psyche, which serve as checks on these instinctual demands. These are the ego and the super-ego. On the face of it, then, the Freudian system would seem to involve an authoritarian régime, necessitating the building up of internal restraints through external pressure of an almost Wesleyan fierceness. The romantic belief in the unrestricted efflorescence of personality as the ethically 'right' mode of development, would seem to be repudiated. Freud's is essentially the tragic view of the human situation. Yet an examination of the precise rôle assigned to the ego and super-ego shows that the Freudian conception of 'right' development does not imply a simple restrictive or repressive system. This comes about through the split between 'morality' (conscience) and rationality. As Niebuhr puts it, 'Freud's science has invalidated the idea of a god-like reason, which can and does impose duty on inclination'; rationalist he may have remained; but the relation of 'reason' and 'duty' was profoundly altered. Indeed, the ego often needs reinforcement against the peremptory demands of the moral nature; for it stands between the id and the super-ego, and suffers from the encroachments of *both*. The super-ego, which represents the introjection of the parent figures, becomes the seat of conscience and exercises the censorship of morals:

> As the child was once compelled to obey its parents, so the ego submits to the categorical imperative pronounced by its super-ego. (*The Ego and the Id*)

Now it is true that the super-ego has a job of great importance in 'civilizing' individuals:

> Civilization therefore obtains the mastery over the dangerous love of aggression in individuals by enfeebling it and disarming it and setting up an institution within their minds to keep watch over it, like a garrison in a conquered city. (*Civilization and its Discontents*)

From the renunciation enforced by the super-ego, guilt develops; and as pain is an essential if unpleasant necessity for the continuance of bodily existence, so guilt is essential for the survival of social life. But there exists an optimum degree of restrictive power at the disposal of the super-ego which avoids, on the one hand, the moral anarchy which would result from too little development and on the other the crippling of psychic life which springs from its overstimulation. Freud discovered that man could be *too* moral; too great stricture could be crippling.

Freud and Education

The excoriations of conscience are, of course, a not infrequent subject for novelists; a major theme in Henry James, for example, involves refinements of moral awareness leading to renunciation. But though James was aware, particularly towards the latter part of his career, of the conflicts between renunciation and the injunction to 'live', his fine moral perceptiveness, in his greatest work, approved the renunciation of an Isabel Archer or a Fleda Vetch. His near contemporary, Freud, only thirteen years his junior, moves nearer, in the name of hedonism, to a tempered indulgence. The super-ego in fact, has two faults:

> . . . in commanding and prohibiting with such severity it troubles too little about the happiness of the ego, and it fails to take into account sufficiently the difficulties in the way of obeying it—the strength of instinctual cravings in the id and the hardships of external environment. (*Civilization and its Discontents*)

The hair shirt, then, is no longer a sign of superior morality, but the mark of an over-repressive conscience. 'Mental health' demands its abandonment. The instinctual strivings demand a degree of recognition.

Thus Freud's attitude to the moral agency in man is equivocal. He admits that the 'strengthening of the super-ego is a highly valuable psychological possession for culture'. But, at the same time, as a result of his clinical experience, he urges that 'in our therapy we often find ourselves obliged to do battle with the super-ego and work to moderate its demands'. Renunciation itself may stimulate the super-ego, because though renunciation of gratification has taken place, the wish persists and cannot be hidden from the super-ego: 'every renunciation becomes a dynamic fount of conscience'.

One cannot help noting, in Freud's own attitude and in its repercussions, a certain moral coarsening. Of course, in saying this, one must step lightly. Undoubtedly the puritan conscience in certain of its manifestations can be an unpleasing thing, and in some cases a crippling one. Obsessive acts can, undoubtedly, spring from an overstimulated conscience, and Freud's remarks must be understood in relation to his clinical experience. At the same time, my reference to Henry James above was not fortuitous; it was a preparatory means of indicating as a sort of 'touchstone' a degree of moral refinement, displayed by James in his novels and stories, which Freud nowhere reveals. Indications of a comparative moral obtuseness emerge from Freud's references to literature and religion. His comments on religion in *The Future of an Illusion* are often depressingly naïve; and it is a shock to read, in Lecture 23 of the *Introductory Lectures*, of the artist as 'one who is urged on by instinctual needs which are too clamorous: he loves to attain to honour, power, riches, fame and the love of woman'. Such a notion is basically vulgar; and it is vulgar because of a lack of moral insight into the nature of the true artist's integrity. Such a judgment is made the more perplexing when one considers Freud's own genuine interest in and admiration for literature.

Freud, too, sometimes speaks as if the 'real' personality is manifested only in the cruder instinctual strivings. For example, in his *Introductory Lectures* he tells of a young man's relation to his father—one of outward piety, involving tender ministrations during the father's protracted illness but, if a dream analysis is to be believed, masking an unconscious antagonism. Freud comments on the latter state of affairs:

> I have no doubt that this was, *in reality*, his attitude towards his father during the protracted illness and that his ostentatious assertions of filial piety were designed to divert his mind from any recollections of the sort. (my italics)

Such a diagnosis involves a moral crudening of the whole situation, a reduction to a lower moral level. The piety, after all, is as 'real' as the antagonism, for it constitutes the civilizing 'form' which controls the more primitive urges. Freud once asserted: 'The Unconscious is the true psychical reality'. Thus, the psychically 'real' tends to be equated with those primitive strivings, those crude instinctual urges it is the function of civilization largely to control and repress. I believe that this tendency to equate the true psychic 'reality' with the primitive rather than with the 'moral' self has been profoundly influential in our era, especially in its literature. It has induced a whole new school of 'realist' writers, especially in America, to prefer passion and the exploitation of crude behaviour to the examination of moral sensibility. There is, of course, another side to Freud; but there is no doubt but that he was mightily fascinated by the id: and in this our age has followed him all too readily.

In thus drawing attention to this lack of moral refinement in Freud's outlook, this lack of a certain sensibility, I in no way mean to detract from the immense genius of his achievement; after all, the sorts of dilemmas inherent in psychoanalytic treatment are often—though not always—of a comparatively crude type; and, indeed, one can see that a certain obtuseness of moral sensibility, a certain lack of delicacy would be an essential prerequisite for anyone, particularly at that time, who was proposing to visit those dark nights of the soul revealed during analytic treatment. The coarsening process is an inevitable concomitant of the immense positive achievement of therapy. Moreover, one can see that a lack of involvement is a necessary element in a therapeutic situation. Scientific detachment in human relations necessarily exacts a certain price. And in defence of Freud, one can easily detect the total ineffectiveness of a Henry James as a practising analyst. Nevertheless, this relative obtuseness of Freud—if granted—has important repercussions.

For one detects in Freud the acceptance, as norm, of a comparatively crude conception of 'l'homme moyen sensuel'. The images he uses are not without their significance in this respect:

> Our mind . . . is no peacefully self-contained unity. It is rather to be compared to a modern State in which a mob, eager for enjoyment and destruction, has to be held down forcibly by a prudent superior class. (*Collected Papers*, Vol. 5.)

In view of the image of 'the mob', it is not surprising to find that in Freud, love often seems to be a matter of instinctual libidinous desire and not a matter of the totally engaged sensibilities; the notion is of a conflict between vulgar desire and inherently superior reason, not of their mutual interaction and emergence as what Wordsworth calls the 'feeling intellect'. Again, the phenomenon of tenderness is not one that Freud much refers to; as Philip Rieff points out, he never 'understood the ethics of self-sacrifice'. The mechanistic model of psychic change referred to above, involving 'discharge' of excitations according to the law of constancy, reveals, perhaps, a source of his crudity. The norm, for Freud, is not one of living at the height of the moment, sensitivities totally and reciprocally engaged, but a state of equilibrium, of neutrality in hard separateness from 'harsh' reality—significant epithet, as we shall see. The pleasure-seeking instinctual urges display no capacity for altruism or self-transcendence, but achieve only discharge or repression. For Freud man stands over against 'reality' like a sullen animal kept at bay by a big stick. Even the repressed, in the unconscious, is never forgotten but remains ever ready to express its bitterness and resentment.

Along with this goes a somewhat equivocal attitude to 'civilization'. His view of the civilized life is, in the main, materialistic, despite a not insincere obeisance in the direction of 'beauty'. At the same time, he often talks as if he realizes the vital importance of instinctual renunciation, through repression or sublimation, as a means to social life; such renunciations become 'the source . . . of the grandest cultural achievements, which are brought to birth by ever greater sublimation of the components of the sexual instinct'. Nor is this an isolated reference to the benefits and achievements of civilization. One of the difficulties, however, of interpreting Freud, with his immense output of written papers and books, lies in the fact that he often expresses conflicting opinions. Thus, he is capable of saying categorically:

> . . . we have found it impossible to give our support to conventional sexual morality or to approve highly of the means by which society attempts to arrange the practical problems of sexuality in life. (*Introductory Lectures*)

And again:

> It need not be said that a culture which leaves unsatisfied and drives to rebelliousness so large a number of its members

neither has the prospect of continued existence, nor deserves it.
(*Future of an Illusion*)

Here, one begins to sense the equivocal part played by Freud's hedonism—a hedonism which, as we have noted, expresses itself as an absence of stimulation rather than as a positive state of euphoria, as an itch to be got rid of rather than a creative thing. Although well aware that some degree of renunciation is an essential prerequisite to any form of life in society, he seems only partially convinced that the achievements of civilization are worth the dessication (as he considers it) involved. Whereas in his picture of man, he is in sharp opposition to the rationalistic optimism of his age, in this he is much more at one with it. Since happiness replaced salvation as the commonly accepted goal, any form of asceticism or any restrictions on the expression of self other than in purely social terms have seemed irrelevant at best and perverse at worst. Hence Freud's unease at the fact of renunciation, despite his awareness of the daemonic force of instinctual demand. One senses, in the background of the Freudian ethic, the modern assumption that fullness of life has a quantitative—Freud would have called it an 'economic'—not a qualitative, connotation. One would put it another way by saying that much of the experience of, say, Eliot's *Four Quartets*, would seem strange to him despite the austerity of his own life.

Freud's analysis of the ego reinforces our dissatisfaction. The ego brings the influence of the external world to bear upon the id and tries to substitute the reality-principle for the pleasure-principle. It represents 'what we call reason and sanity'. One of its main characteristics is its weakness, a weakness implied in the similes Freud uses in referring to it:

> The ego's position is like that of a constitutional monarch, without whose sanction no law can be passed but who hesitates long before imposing a veto on any measure put forward by parliament (*The Ego and the Id*).

Hence

> Its position mid-way between the id and reality tempts it only too often to become sycophantic, opportunist and false,

like a politician who sees the truth but wants to keep his place in popular favour (*The Ego and the Id*).

It is little wonder, then, that Freud emphasizes the importance of the affective life in psychic development. The ego appears weak and uncertain in its behaviour, its control all too easily upset by the peremptory demands of the id, or crushed by the hyper-moral demands of the super-ego.

Yet it is at the strengthening of the ego that the therapeutic process aims. It is, as I have noted above, a quite fundamental mistake to think of Freud as an irrationalist. He realized the strength of the irrational side of man's nature, and the precarious nature of his conquest of the passional id. But the aim of therapy was to replace the 'consequences of repression by rational mental effort'. 'The voice of the intellect is a soft one, but it does not rest until it has gained a hearing', he said in *The Future of an Illusion*. He described it as 'reclamation work, like the draining of the Zuyder Zee', its object being

> to strengthen the ego, to make it more independent of the super-ego, to widen its field of vision, and so to extend its organization that it can take over new portions of the id (*New Introductory Lectures*).

He sums up: 'Where id was, there ego shall be.' Or, to put it another way, the essence of psychoanalytic therapy is 'reality testing'.

It is when we ask what 'reality' meant to Freud that the dissatisfaction I have referred to receives its confirmation. Lionel Trilling has, to some extent, drawn attention to these unsatisfactory features in his essay in *The Liberal Imagination* on 'Freud and Literature'. Trilling admits that what crudeness exists in Freud's conception of 'reality' no doubt in part stems from the comparative rawness of the analytic situation. As the unrealities of neurotic patients are often of a not very subtle kind, therapy is 'aimed not at theoretical refinement but at practical effectiveness. The polar extremes are practical reality and neurotic illusion'. Yet, he continues, the ' "reality" inherent in Freud's therapeutic purpose is one that is wholly "given", something quite fixed and static, not something that is essentially, in the Coleridgean phrase, the product of a coalescence of subject and object', or, in the word of Dewey's that Trilling quotes, one that is 'taken'. This is largely, one conjectures, because Freud's world of reality is one based on purely scientific criteria: 'Scientific work is our only way to the knowledge of external reality'. For the aim of science is

> to arrive at correspondence with reality, that is to say with what exists outside us and independently of us, and, as experience has taught us, is decisive for the fulfilment or frustration of our desires (*New Introductory Lectures*).

Thus it is not surprising to find Freud assuming that part of the function of the ego is to afford a 'picture' of reality somewhat in the passive mode of a camera, in order to persuade the id to avoid a suicidal demand for complete satisfaction in face of superior external forces:

> In the fulfilment of this function, the ego has to observe the external world and preserve a true picture of it in the memory traces left by its perceptions, and by means of the reality-test, it has to eliminate any element in this picture of the external world which is a contribution from internal sources of excitation.

In other words, the ego is purely passive in perception; it simply presents to the straining and impatient id a true image of the 'reality' it has to face in seeking satisfaction; it *accepts* stimuli and only then does it actively react.

> The relation of the ego to the outer world is passive in so far as it receives stimuli from it, active when it reacts to these. Its instincts compel it to a quite special degree of activity towards the outside world, so that, . . . we might say that the ego-subject is passive in respect of external stimuli, active in virtue of its own instincts (*Instincts and their Vicissitudes*).

Furthermore, this 'reality', is always looked upon as 'harsh', as I have noted above. So, of course, it must have seemed to many of Freud's patients. But Freud's work has a connotation outside the clinical relationship of therapist and patient and so the implications of his words must be considered. The world is, for Freud, never a thing of joyous acceptance—nor is it one where, the 'controls' function positively as well as negatively.

Freud and Education

Hence Freud's curiously ambivalent attitude to art and literature. For all his admiration and respect for the artist, in the last analysis Freud thought of him as the provider of substitute gratifications. Art provides compensation—or at most therapy —rather than a means of apprehending features of the 'real' world through the exacting use of certain media. In this way, art becomes a matter of relaxation rather than an incredibly difficult 'form' of apprehension leading to a profounder appreciation of the external world and to some enjoyment of it. Art Freud said, 'does not seek to be anything else but an illusion'. At best, the artist occupies 'the intermediate territory between the wish-denying reality and the wish-fulfilling world of phantasy'.

Implicit in Freud's concern for 'education to reality', his aim to strengthen the ego as a matter of therapy, there lurks, of course, a moral ideal. As A. C. MacIntyre puts it:

> Freud's whole recognition of unconscious purposes is a discovery that men are more, and not less, rational than we thought they were. His whole method of treatment rests on an assertion that men can face and cope with their situation rationally, if only they are given the opportunity. Freud himself helps to conceal this from us by his vehement disavowal of any moralistic purpose in his work. Nonetheless he promotes a moral ideal for which rationality is central (*The Unconscious*).

It is interesting, nevertheless, to note how often Freud denied a *specifically* moral aim, in the sense that he was unwilling to recommend any *specific* course of action to patients. Indeed, a course of therapy often assumes an atmosphere of complete permissiveness. 'We are not reformers; . . . we are merely observers,' was Freud's way of putting it. In his *Introductory Lectures*, he urges that

> . . . you are quite misinformed if you imagine that advice and guidance concerning conduct in life forms an integral part of the analytic method. On the contrary, as far as possible, we refrain from playing the part of mentor; we want nothing better than that the patient should find his own solutions for himself.

At the same time, it is as well to remember that, however

56

permissive the analytic situation may seem to be, the very meeting of doctor and patient implies an inequality of rôles, and an orientation of the patient to the analyst of a qualitatively different nature from that of the analyst to the patient. The analyst's authority is not less real for being indirect; and, as I have noted before, the analytic pact implies a moral aim of increased rationality, a conquest of ego over id. It is not surprising, then, to find Freud himself referring on one occasion, to psycho-analytic treatment as a 'kind of re-education'.

II

I must consider now the implications of the lack of moral refinement inherent in the Freudian view, and the feeling of dissatisfaction I have with Freud's views on 'reality'; the relevance of my analysis to education and mental health I want to make clear. An element of moral debility has crept into 'progressive' schooling through its emphasis on relaxation, its concern to remove tensions, its frequent indifference to notions of achievement, its hostility to externally imposed standards, its continual and excessive emphasis on the importance of personal relationships in the classroom and its comparative lack of interest in the creative forces built up by a common, impersonally generated pursuit of objective learning. Some of these manifestations are part of the mental health movement too. Thus there is certainly an anti-intellectual bias;[1] and there is the excessive distrust, generated by too strong an emphasis on possible 'unconscious motivations', so that the conscientious become inhibited and introverted; for when may not rationality be rationalization? Although there have been other influences at work, one cannot help feeling that Freud's hedonism, together with his views of human fulfilment in essentially negative terms of discharge of tensions, attainment of equilibrium, fulfilment of the law of constancy, has contributed to this state of affairs. The permissiveness of the analytic session has been thought relevant to the classroom. Here, often, successful living implies a

[1] Cf. 'The School and Mental Health' pp. 40–42.

state of nullity, an absence of stimulation, an escape from tension; and human creativity involves not a bitter, perpetually renewed, demonic, immensely joyous struggle with intractable material and media, through which man achieves some measure of control and transcendency over the internal and external worlds and thus reaches what Ortega Y Gasset calls 'the height of the times', but a release, an acquiescence in harsh reality, a mere therapeutic exercise.[1] The teacher must be passive, must 'accept'. He should not demand. 'Reality' is, as I have noted, something to come to terms with, not something to 'conquer'. And we must remember that the view of 'reality' we consciously or unconsciously accept subtly interpenetrates our vision of the world, which is itself in part the creation of the assumptions in terms of which we interpret what we see.

There is, also, the danger that too much emphasis on Freudianism will cruden our psychic life by associating the crude and harsh with the real. This has already to some extent happened in literature as I have briefly mentioned; but the diffusion of a half-knowledge—which is all it could possibly be—through the licensing of teachers to undertake any sort of therapeutic rôle, the further promulgation of those glib diagnostic formulations one recognizes only too well in the mouths of those who have assimilated the Freudian smatterings, would introduce into an essentially 'normal' situation with its own 'reality' quite undesirable pathological formulations. In the previous essay I quoted a remark by Dr. Halmos deprecating attention to the 'G.C.E.O.' when a child is having 'nightmares every night'.[2] It is as well to remember that the G.C.E. is as much part of life as the nightmares—and, for all its inadequacies as an examination, a healthier part. If the nightmares persist, specialized treatment is called for; but it could hardly be seriously suggested that in the teaching situation the teacher should introduce the pathological situation to the rest of the class rather than the—to them—

---

[1] One of the reasons often given for creative work and drama in schools is that such work will encourage release from tension. The specifically creative *struggle* seems to be forgotten.

[2] Cf. p. 41.

more real, and healthier, concern for the examination. Even when everything has been said about the faults of examinations, there is nothing pathological in acquiring knowledge for passing them; the outgoingness such study involves, even the moral qualities of persistence it invokes, are preferable signs to either the glib knowingness or the self-pity likely to be engendered by half-understood Freud—or even fully understood Freud in some of his guises. My point has been that this moral coarseness which is part—an inevitable part—of the Freudian experience needs most careful handling by an expert, not by a dabbler. And my view receives important confirmation from Professor Bruno Bettelheim as a result of his experiences in a German concentration camp:

> Without any deliberate intention by psychoanalysts, and often contrary to their stated beliefs, the emphasis of nearly all investigations is on what went wrong in people's lives, and what can be done to correct the mishaps. Since psychologists deal with these problems mainly or only, this is entirely legitimate. But it does not then offer a theory giving positive guidance towards a good life. . . .
>
> Psychoanalysts would be among the first to say that the import of their theories and practice now goes well beyond the narrow field of psychotherapy; they are well aware of its importance in sociology, education, aesthetics, life. But when psychoanalysis is thus applied outside the limits of psycho-therapy, then serious hazards may appear if its original point of departure, and its continual emphasis on the morbid, and the pathological are not tempered by equally careful attention to the healthy, the normal, the positive. Through such concentration on the bad and its correction, one could easily arrive at a theory according to which overcoming the morbid rather than its absence, becomes the norm of a healthy personality (*The Informed Heart*).

Who, indeed, would blame the Freud of psychoanalysis for this? His world, after all, is the world of morbid states and diseased psyches, and his recipe that for a bare minimum of rational existence; it should not be accepted as a norm of human possibilities and potentialities, such as the school is concerned to foster. For the school's job is with refinement, not therapy.

Freud and Education

We have indeed fundamentally mistaken Freud's purpose; and he himself has helped our mis-interpretation by venturing, like so many in our times, into fields where he has no necessary competence to speak. His scientific work, crude though it will inevitably seem after another hundred years, as seems all the scientific work of even the greatest earlier scientists, nevertheless places him among the supreme scientific geniuses of all time, the equivalent of Copernicus, Newton, Darwin and Einstein. His model of the functioning of the human psyche has enabled him to exercise a measure of control over morbid states which entitles him to the gratitude and plaudits of mankind. My attempt to sort out and distinguish the rôles of teacher and therapist implies no disrespect whatsoever for the therapist. But such a model has no necessary connection with normal states and is, indeed, even in connection with diseased states, a mere construct, an artifact which serves a limited purpose of 'explaining' a range of psychic phenomena; just as in its day the billiard ball model of the atom served to clarify, at the then stage of knowledge, the findings of the physicists. One of the curses of psycho-analysis has been its popularity; and Freud has been treated as a seer, instead of as a genius in a strictly limited sphere. On the whole, I cannot help thinking it would have been a good thing if psycho-analysis had remained as esoteric a matter as modern somatic medicine, understood as requiring a highly specialized training and left alone by the laity. The teacher, indeed, might be encouraged to know as much in the field of psycho-analysis as he is at present taught about health education, and no more.

Perhaps the most useful thing that the teacher could learn from Freud would be to leave alone or treat with care and delicacy certain aspects of children's behaviour—in many instances seeking expert diagnosis rather than accepting rough rule-of-thumb methods which have served the school-master throughout the centuries. Just as the most ordinary teacher will usually treat gently the bilious child with an upset stomach, so he ought to learn to tread gently with certain behavioural problems which formerly he would have regarded as within his province. For example, sexual mis-behaviour among children should be treated with care and circumspection, and in case of persistence expert advice should be sought. The phenomenon of persistent and prolonged 'naughtiness' should be regarded as the complex manifestation of inner disharmony it is and again, where necessary, psychotherapeutic treatment provided. Some understanding of the possible affective interferences with cognition and learning in general should be given so that sudden fallings off in effectiveness of apprehension can be investigated, or backwardness more successfully diagnosed.[1] Freud provides further confirmatory evidence of that belief which the progressives have held from at least the time of Rousseau, that the child has urges and desires within him which must be allowed for when teaching him; particularly has he confirmed beliefs in the vital importance of the earlier years, when the ambivalence of the child's feelings needs particularly sympathetic handling. Where these young children are concerned, the traditional good infant teacher's combination of sympathy and firmness has received confirmation: it is a commonplace that Freud gives no support to the extreme libertarianism which was popular among progressives some time ago. Susan Isaacs herself makes this perfectly clear in words which have been strangely neglected: thus, in emphasizing the elements of phantasy and tension which accompanied the early phases, emerging often as outbursts of hate and desstructiveness—implicit in Freud's own formulations of instincts—she drew attention to the rôle of the 'good, strict parent' in the upbringing of even the youngest children and repudiates any idea of complete freedom, supposing such were attainable:

> What the child actually needs is that the parents and the adults who make up his social world should represent to him a stable and ordered world of values, values closely related to the child's real abilities at any given age, and based upon an understanding of his psychological needs, but which are, nevertheless, firm and unwavering in themselves. Young children do need

[1] In other words, teachers can be helped to *recognise*; they should not be expected to *explain*.

Freud and Education

to feel that the adults around them are stronger than themselves and represent, not the forces of destruction, but those of ordered creation (*Social Development*).

I hope that, by now, the nature of my plea will be sufficiently clear. Freud's theories have magnificently helped certain types of people suffering from a limited range of psychic disorders; their efficacy there is manifest if not totally undisputed. In other spheres, their value is much more open to question. His model of psychic equilibrium has its relevance within a restricted sphere because, at the present stage of discovery, it has its explanatory uses; even here, it may in time be superseded. Elsewhere, its application is highly disputable and may even be unfortunate. His morality may be reasonably adequate to many of the crude dilemmas of neurotic obsession; elsewhere it is coarsely inadequate. Where the work of the educator is concerned, a similar drawing of boundaries is necessary. The teacher's relationship with the child is defined in terms of the limited endeavour arising out of the transmission of skills, knowledge and refinement of feeling. It is only when the psychically 'odd' or 'unusual'—within the meaning of the terms implied above—is encountered that the teacher requires a rough diagnostic power to decide whether the disturbance is rationally explicable in terms of common disappointments or sorrows, or springs from a profounder malaise. If the latter is suspected, he must seek expert help; to assume any therapeutic competence would be at once arrogant and dangerous.[1]

Thus Freud is best regarded as a genius within a strictly limited sphere; any suggestions of competence outside that sphere, though not to be ruled out *ad hoc*, need scrutinizing with the greatest care. In the same way, untrained laymen must not take unto themselves a competence which they simply have not got. Any teacher can aspire to the sensitive insights inherent in great literature; but to assume a technically complex rôle without the training that is its essential pre-requisite would be a grave folly.

[1] Cf. 'The School and Mental Health' pp. 31–35.

Freud and Education

III

Again, in the controversy over emotional education I wish to make my position quite clear. I think there is considerable substance in the re-emphasis that emotional factors play a highly important part in the developing personality. What I deprecate is the implication that many children are unable to control their emotional immaturities by the ordinary accepted means within the conventional world of work and play and without the need to summon the depth psychologist. The suggestion of such a need is subtly undermining to the very sense of personal responsibility which is one of the major achievements of Western civilization. There is, in any case, a distinction between young people who have emotional problems—which are endemic in the human condition—and those who are neurotic; the one can achieve a measure of conscious control and ordering of the personality, the other is in the grip of his disturbance and needs treatment. Translated into educational terms, this intends to urge that most children can be helped to attain some personal ordering of the psyche through the more normal and traditional sources of affective education, the arts; if the others show signs of serious disturbance then they should, as I have suggested above, be sent to the appropriate clinic, in the efficacy of which I have considerable faith.[1]

I would urge, indeed, that the advocates of mental health based on Freudian 'insights' deserve our gratitude to the extent at least that they place squarely before us the need for attention to the affective element in human nature. But the development of most children can be encompassed by a greater attention to the arts and crafts, which mingle the emotional and the intellectual proportionately as means to the control of the self through the particular medium chosen—whether words, paint, stone, clay or simply patterned movement, as in the

[1] On the grounds of personal observation alone I find the objections made by Professor Eysenck quite unacceptable; and I must stress again that I have no reservations whatsoever concerning the possible effectiveness of psychotherapy.

dance. These sources of 'mental health' receive two little attention in our schools, though they lead to that 'very culture of the feelings' one of our greatest intellects, John Stuart Mill, assigned to them. Nor is this to deny the satisfactions which more specifically intellectual pursuits can, of themselves, offer to able children: the effort of thought concentration can be a great emotional calmer.

1958

3

The Education of the Emotions

Emotion, one of the most frequently used, nevertheless remains one of the most elusive terms employed in modern psychology. The origin of the word, according to the O.E.D., is the Latin *emovere*, to move away or remove. The notion of movement seems to be fundamental to the etymology of the word. In earlier usages it could imply a 'moving out, migration', or a physical 'moving, stirring, agitation'; and hence, metaphorically, it could be used to refer to a 'popular movement, tumult'. It then comes to be used figuratively with reference to 'any vehement or excited mental state', and hence to take on its modern psychological meaning as a 'mental feeling or affection (e.g. of pain, hope, desire, etc.) as distinct from volitions and cognitions'.

The basic implication of the word, then, seems to be that it refers to something which involves alterations—however slight —in a person's psychic equilibrium, with possible repercussions on conduct. The occurrence of an emotion, it would seem, does not leave a person unchanged. It may lead him to feel inner feelings of disturbance, with some possible outward manifestations; or it may lead him to alter his conduct—in order, for instance, to take evasive action to avoid the state of affairs which is likely to cause the disturbance. Such a distinction employs the useful division made by Mr. A. Kenny in his *Action, Emotion and Will*, when he discriminates between emotion as feeling and emotion as motive.[1] What they have in common is an effect on

[1] If emotion has implications for conduct, it has, of course, obvious connections with the processes of moral education. At the same time, Mr. Kenny's distinction exists largely for the purpose of analysis—emotion as motive must also exist as feeling, though perhaps not always vice versa.

the potentialities for behaviour of the subject—'potentialities' of behaviour because though they will often manifest themselves in action or conduct the subject may be able to hide or disguise the incidence of his emotion from the eyes of others. What is important, however, is that, as a result of the incidence of the emotion, the 'set' of the individual shall in some degree be altered: the potentiality for movement will be there and it will need a conscious counter-effort to prevent the movement from manifesting itself. Or it may be that it will manifest itself only in thoughts or day-dreams. As Mr. Kenny puts it:

> If John is in love with Mary, then he must in some way or other conduct his life differently from a man who is not in love with Mary. But there seems no reason to think that what is done in such cases must always be something public; perhaps the only upshot of a man's love for a woman may be that he thinks a lot about her. To be sure, in that case, we shall want some explanation why his love goes no further; but such explanations are to be found—perhaps Mary is already happily married (p. 64).

If, then, thoughts or day-dreams can be included under the heading of behaviour, though of a non-observable type, much emotion involves that sort of 'movement' appropriate to human beings which we term conduct.

Once it is admitted that emotion may manifest itself in some sort of conduct, whether internal or having outward characteristics, the incidence of emotion comes to be subject to ethical judgment; and this is signalized in the extent to which emotion has often been regarded with some suspicion. This is implicit in some of the earlier definitions of the word, which have involved the notion of agitation or tumult. Many theories of emotion have thought of it as a sort of energy; it has been conceived on the analogy of electricity in a circuit or water in a pipe; and the metaphor has been carried on in implications of the need to regulate or control the 'flow'. Thus frequently the notion of excess has come to be associated with manifestations of emotion; we speak of someone 'giving way to his emotions', usually with a slightly pejorative implication. Emotions, then, become forms

The Education of the Emotions

of energy which need to be held in check—as in the famous image in Plato's *Phaedrus* of the charioteer with two horses, one white and good and amenable to reason and the other dark and ungovernable. Or we speak of an overpowering emotion or of being in the grip of our emotions, both of which imply some notion of excess, with the suggestion that conduct which occurs during such a situation may not be altogether desirable or even healthy; we speak of the need to reduce the emotional 'temperature'.

All this implies some sort of regulating device. But, before I examine further what is suggested, it is important to note that not all take this view of the need to check emotion. Indeed, it is clear that all such views stem from a particular ethical ideal rather than from an empirical psychology. Two conceptions of man struggle for mastery in European thought: there is the rational ideal which tends to identify man with what is regarded as most truly characteristic of him—his reason. In this view, emotion is in part regarded as an aberration, and those ways of speaking of it I have just noted tend to occur. But there are also those who see man most truly himself in his expressions of emotion, when emotion becomes the essence of life: where emotion is, life is. Man is most truly himself in his ebullitions of passion, and the rational is equated with the conventional or the uninspiring.

Now, related to these two different conceptions are two regulating devices—two conceptions of therapy. In the case of the one, the attempt is to achieve rationality, as in psycho-analysis, where the idea is to get rid of the emotion:

> The aim is separation (analysis) of the elements, a rational method having for its results dispassionate ideas and images on one side and motor discharge of emotion on the other. It is an ethic for the sake of intellect and will, where action, decision, peaceful order and rational planning are the goals. It is a therapy of representations, curing representations of their emotional attachments. It is not a therapy of emotion, curing emotions of their fixated images.[1]

[1] J. Hillman: *Emotion*, pp. 179–180.

The Education of the Emotions

The issue here is to increase rationality and decrease emotion; what is achieved is homeostasis, a reassertion of equilibrium. But, in the other theory, the attempt (regulating device) is to harness and perhaps refine emotion, to transform it, for instance, by the organization of affect through symbolization. This is a therapeutic device used by Jungian psychologists. Through the development of symbolic forms the emotion also is developed— 'tamed'; hence the arts, religious ceremonies, etc. employ but transform the emotions: 'through the careful elaboration and refinement of these symbols, there takes place an educative, aesthetic and moral process.' (Op.cit., pp. 183–184).

What is perhaps not altogether clear, in the latter case, is why, if one lives most truly in emotion, emotion should need 'refining' or regulation. Both theories, indeed, seem to rest on the assumption that the expression of what might be termed 'raw' emotion is somehow undesirable. In the one case it is to be 'discharged', in the other it is to be ordered, articulated and refined: for

> the extraordinary thing about emotion is not its highly dubious single root, but its actual phenomenology, its incredible range and shifting variety. And so the direction of therapy would not be downward and backward towards the extraction of some root, the extinction of some evil essence; instead it would aim towards the full play and free flowering of emotional life, still the mark of heroes in human culture.[1]

A clue to the discrepancy is surely contained in the first sentence concerning the actual phenomenology of the emotions; they have an incredible range and variety. The tendency has been to categorize them as being of a homogeneous type or as having a common function, manifest in behaviour of a certain type which has then attracted ethical attention and been condemned or approved of in accordance with moral presuppositions. Emotions have encountered notions of bad form, social disapproval which, in certain circles, has frowned on displays of feeling; the general ethos of our civilization has, through its emphasis on scientific criteria of 'truth', encouraged cognition of a peculiarly un-emotional kind as the paradigm of successful approaches to the

[1] Hillman: op.cit., p. 165.

The Education of the Emotions

world. It is not surprising, then, that the emotions have tended to have a bad press and that, even when approved, have been thought to be in need of refinement.

Actual observation would seem to suggest that the 'emotions' manifest themselves in a variety of ways and fulfil a variety of functions and purposes. The mistake of homogenizing them is encouraged by the way in which we speak of *the* emotions', as if they formed a homogeneous collection of phenomena which could all be categorized in the same way. After all, we do not speak of the 'cognitions', for it is obvious that cognition manifests itself in a number of different ways—as recognition, deduction from stated or assumed axioms, induction from observation, insightful leap, reconstruction of basic models, and so on. One speaks of 'knowing' that $2 + 2 = 4$, that objects heavier than air fall in a vacuum at a uniform rate of acceleration, that my Redeemer liveth, though very different criteria of judgment are presupposed by all these acts of apprehension which are brought together under the general heading of 'knowing'. In the same way, emotions may accompany, or overwhelm, or make one aware of, or fail to materialize when expected, or even conflict; and one may 'feel' that such and such is the case, or a desire, or simply numb.

In general, the two fields of emotion and cognition have been thought of as separate and often opposed; the calmness of intellect has been contrasted with the turbulence of emotion despite the fact that the initial focussing of attention which the exercise of intellect requires is presumably of emotional origin. We need, under such circumstances, to concentrate the attention; and the very notion of concentration implies that marshalling of powers, that movement and focussing of mentality which imply some element of affect.[1]

Ordinary speech, indeed, confirms this imputation of an affective element in the performance even of highly intellectual

---

[1] 'Only the psychology that has separated things which in reality belong together holds that scientists and philosophers think while poets and painters follow their feelings. In both . . . there is emotionalized thinking, and there are feelings whose substance consists of appreciated meanings or ideas.' (Dewey: *Art as Experience*, p. 73, (1958).)

activities. We speak, for instance, of our attention being gripped or rivetted, both of which words imply the forcefulness and power one associates with the emotions. Furthermore, both words imply something else which is very typical of emotional manifestations, an external agency; one is gripped by something, attention is riveted or focused on something. In some manifestations of emotion, at least, the world outside the self plays an important part. States of emotion certainly do not always arise out of subjective states of mind; they can clearly be stimulated or aroused by objects or states in the external world. Not only may emotion be said to *accompany* modes of pure cognition; it may constitute the form taken by certain modes of understanding, certain acts of cognition.

That many manifestations of emotion are closely related to 'objects' (which may include situations) in the external world seems undeniable:

> It is possible to be hungry without being hungry for anything in particular, as it is not possible to be ashamed without being ashamed of anything in particular.[1]

In general when we employ emotion-words, we imply not simply hope or fear or love but something of which we are afraid, something we hope for, someone we love. Emotions, then, can have objects; they may involve a way of responding to the environment. As Sartre says: 'Emotion is a certain way of apprehending the world'.

Sartre's theory of emotion forms an interesting contrast to those who consider that emotion is something which is suffered or undergone, which involves a passivity on the part of the sufferer. I am walking along a street when suddenly I meet a lion. I am terrified; I stand rooted to the spot, unable to move; or else I faint. In both cases I am overwhelmed by my fear. I am no longer a reasoning being capable of action; instead I am so much in the grip of my fears that I can do nothing. I suffer a total disablement, I am as if acted upon by forces beyond my power to control, I am made passive by my terror.

Sartre's account of such a situation would differ. He would

[1] Kenny: op.cit., p. 60.

make of such strong emotion an act of consciousness, not simply a suffering. Admittedly it would be unreflective, but it would, nevertheless, be purposive, a mode of action, a means of dealing with the situation, not simply an acceptance of it. Its purpose would be to annihilate my difficulties by magically transforming the world; the magic would consist of the fact that my action on myself—fainting—is intended as transformation of the world, not of myself. It is a way of denying the presence of the lion; the threat is annihilated, the world transformed. Such emotional transformation of the world means that a magical universe supersedes the instrumental or pragmatic one we inhabit normally:

> When the paths traced out become too difficult, or when we see no path, we can no longer live in so urgent or difficult a world. All the ways are barred. However, we must act. So we try to change the world, that is, to live as if the connection between things and their potentialities were not ruled by deterministic processes, but by magic.[1]

Of course, as Sartre admits, the attempted transformation is a failure; it is in any case quite unreflective. Furthermore, the world is not ruled by magic; we cannot transform it in this way. At first sight, it seems a silly analysis.

Nevertheless, it appears to me to possess some interesting features which to some extent support Sartre's notion that emotion on occasions at least involves an *act* rather than a suffering or a passivity, even where an extreme emotion of this kind is involved. The emotion, for instance, incorporates some degree of assessment of the situation; lions are rightfully regarded as fear-provoking animals. My reaction is not so much an attempt to transform the world as a recognition of the fact that it has been transformed. The innocent passageway along which I was proceeding has suddenly undergone a change; the world has altered and the fear I feel has assessed the nature of this change correctly—at least so far as my limited knowledge of lions goes. My emotion, then, is correctly defined by Sartre as a way of being in the world; it involves an assessment of the

[1] Quoted in Joseph P. Fell III: *Emotion in the Thought of Sartre*, p. 16.

object which is in line with my recognition of it and of the contexts in which previously I have come to understand the concept 'lion'. It is only the excess of fear which makes me faint that seems in some doubt, that seems to involve a passivity. Why don't I take rational steps to escape? then my fear would act as a positive spur, warning me positively to beware with incredible and praiseworthy rapidity. Far from being a passivity, the fear would enable me to assess the situation far more rapidly than a purely cognitive assessment could possibly do; it would prove an essential part of the total act of assessment.

But why do I faint? It is at least plausible to suggest that this may be the result of a limited or imperfect rational cognition. The lion, after all, is an extremely potent symbol; I may think it impossible to escape one and my fainting is simply a way of accepting this fact. Again, my emotion is simply a means of registering an act of recognition—lion, the inescapable. My death is assured. Why delay?

But, in fact, my recognition of the lion is imperfect. I have forgotten those lion tamers who can control the beasts by fixing them with their eyes. Furthermore, my cognition of lions is inadequate. In fact, they are lazy animals and will rarely attack unless hungry. I should therefore be keeping my eyes fixed and trying to note signs of satiety. This, of course, is a perfectly possible reaction, just as possible as fainting.

Now, though my analysis involves certain differences of stress in comparison with that of Sartre, it employs certain elements of Sartre's view. Emotions are directed towards objects; they are ways of apprehending the world. But they are not (necessarily) ways of transforming the world; they may be ways of recognizing transformations *in* the world. Sartre's error springs from the fact that he recognizes only two ways of dealing with the world—the instrumental-pragmatic and the magical. He persists, also, in finding the latter way a self-deceptive one, an inferior unreflective way, and thus aligns himself, ultimately, with those who stress the inferiority of emotion. What he fails to recognize is that the world and its objects may be fearful or lovable, and that emotion may involve a way of apprehending

The Education of the Emotions

the truth about the world and its objects and situations. Furthermore, he calls the emotional view of the world unreflective. In
fact, it is closely bound up with cognition, which may be simply
recognition or an extremely rapid—so rapid as to appear almost
instantaneous—reflective assessment of the situation, when the
fear itself is inextricably involved in the act of assessment.
Emotion, then, can manifest itself as an act or an inextricable
part of an act of consciousness and not simply a suffering. Indeed, expression of emotion can reveal a truth about a situation
which rationality may ignore or, in extreme cases, even be
trying to hide; the lion might spring while the pros and cons of
the situation were being weighed up. Anger or fear, far from
being impositions, sufferings, may be correct ways of dealing
with situations. One's jitters may be more revelatory than one's
cooler arguments.

Let us examine a speech of Macbeth from this point of view.
Macbeth is considering whether or not to kill the king. He
opens with arguments which may be said to weigh the possibilities, to assess the situation rationally:

> If it were done when 'tis done, then 'twere well
> It were done quickly.

If only, he continues, there were no possible repercussions; if
only the murder would prove an end. But I might teach others
a lesson, so that they might do to me what I want to do to
Duncan. It all seems very calculating.

But it isn't—not altogether. Certainly there is an element of
calculation, as the words bring out; but the precise words bring
out something else. Macbeth is frightened; he is in an emotional
state, as even a most superficial examination of the words and
rhythms he employs brings out. The tension is everywhere
apparent, but as yet under some sort of control. But gradually
the control breaks down; the rhythms and imagery become
increasingly hysterical. He who has seemed with such ease to
jump the life to come becomes overwhelmed with images of
heaven and damnation. The fear, the awe, the apprehension
which revealed themselves in an undercurrent of tension to the

initial argument have broken out and totally absorbed his attention. Now, this hysteria could be regarded as a suffering. But, in fact, it reveals the truth of the situation to an extent that the former argument did not. It is not only subjectively revealing about the state of Macbeth's mind. It also reveals an element about the objective situation which reason could not fully assess. The arguments against committing the crime display a narrow assessment of people which judges them in terms applicable to his own behaviour; what I do, others may. Other people are as mean as I am and may serve their own selfish interests in the same way. These are in line with his feelings of ambition and the self-regard such feelings engender. But he is subject to other emotions which arise out of an infinitely grander conception of the realities of the world, where virtues transcend, where pity, for all its apparent frailty, becomes one of the forces of the universe. The emotion sensed in the earlier passage becomes articulated through a set of commonly accepted symbols which force an admission of truth on several levels. 'I have no spur' reveals his own state to himself; his ambition *is* a form of untruth. But this is a consequence of metaphysical dreads and fears which reveal what, in fact, does emerge as the outcome of the play ... the horrid deed *is* blown in every eye; tears *do* drown the wind; the whole notion of killing Duncan is a monstrosity. The awareness *evolved out of the feelings*, articulated as a result of dread and awe, reveal the true state of affairs to Macbeth, if he but had the sense to attend to it. In this case, cognition *arises out of* emotion, *arises out of, as a result of* fears and dreads; and emotion as feeling is translated into emotion as potential motive. Such dreads and fears were part and parcel of man's apprehension of reality at the time the play was written, and evoke an echo of remembrance in our own day.

An 'echo of remembrance' ... why do I here strike the historical note? Because it seems to me that over the last few hundred years the balance of cognition and emotion in the way in which we take the world, in the way in which we apprehend 'reality', has probably altered. Since, in the seventeenth century, 'reality' became increasingly definable in terms of matter-in-motion, the emotions as modes of apprehending the world have suffered a diminution, even an eclipse. Of course, emotions and feelings, to be communicable, have always needed to be articulated, translated into symbols inviting cognition; Macbeth's terror, as I have pointed out, is translated into terms which employ concepts—'angels', 'cherubim'—which form part of a coherent *explanation* of the world in a way which would have been looked on as knowledge about the world in its own times. Nevertheless, the cognitive component serves simply to anchor, to make communicable, and is therefore less important than, the emotional, which here is clearly overwhelming. The cognitive elements are employed emotively, abstracted from the cognitive scheme and used for their affective force. The first words of the whole speech are post Renaissance, post Machiavelli; the later ones look back to a time which apprehended the world in terms of 'energies' rather than concepts, and subordinated its concepts to its awareness of energy.

It is, indeed, one of the basic errors of many writers on the nature of the emotions to posit a split between emotion and cognition. In fact, once expressions of emotion get beyond the primitive evocation of 'oohs' and 'aahs,' grunts and groans, the two are closely inter-involved; it may be that concepts arise out of 'oohs' and 'aahs', provide means of articulating and making comprehensible what moves and disturbs. Or it may be that a frisson arises out of recognition. But it is rare, in conscious human life, to encounter expressions of the one without some use being made of symbols which function in part cognitively.

Yet Sartre, for all the sophistication of his theorizing, splits human experience of reality into two broad categories; our attitude is either emotional and therefore magical, self-deceptive, unreflective and generally inferior; or it is instrumental and therefore perceptive, pragmatic and adjusted to reality as it is. In fact, reality, the world of objects, is much more complex than this sort of talk about it appreciates. For objects may be animate as well as inanimate, and if they are animate, part of their 'reality' is itself emotional or, as Sartre will have it, magical. A purely instrumental approach to such people as objects, will lead one to misconceive them, because part of their reality, affecting their conduct and behaviour, are their own magical awarenesses. This Macbeth implicitly appreciates; reactions are not wholly those of the heavenly powers. The cherubim, it is, he fears,

> shall blow
> The horrid deed in every eye, that tears
> Shall drown the wind.

But the tears are human tears; the reactions to such a deed will involve human feelings of horror, repugnance and sympathy with the wronged king. They are part of the total reality of the deed; the king is not only a concept; he is also involved in a network of feelings, a pattern of responses comprising loyalties and feelings of awe and reverence. These responses need to be apprehended emotionally in order to take on their full force for the assessment of the situation Macbeth is in. That is why his Renaissance calculation of the first part of the speech is inferior *in reality* to his appreciation of the forces at stake in the second half. Feeling, as part of the reality of objects, can only be met by corresponding emotion on the part of the subject. As George Eliot says in *Middlemarch*:

> There is no general doctrine which is not capable of eating out our mortality if unchecked by the deep-seated habit of direct fellow-feeling with individual fellow-men.

This means, as Dorothea discovers in her relationship with Casaubon, treating other people 'as equivalent centres of self'; part of the equivalence implies the capacity for fellow-feeling, for shared emotion, even if its interaction will often employ a set of symbols to form a common currency between both parties.

II

I certainly do not pretend to have given an exhaustive account of the incidence of emotion; but I do claim to have prepared one or two contexts in which it is feasible to consider their *education*. Emotions manifest themselves in different ways and

The Education of the Emotions

fulfil a number of different functions. But in some of their guises, at least, they are means through which we apprehend the world; they tell us about objects; part of their function is informative and they are therefore subject to criteria of truth or falsity. But they are informative in more than one way. They may form part of a process of re-cognition: this is a lion; lions are fierce, they eat people, I am (rightly) afraid. Or they may reveal truths beyond the reach of cold cognition, though translated into symbols and even concepts for the purpose of communication and articulation, truths which recognize one's own feelings and those of others, as Macbeth surrenders to his feelings of awe and terror and his fears of the consequences of such feelings in the minds of others. In both cases feelings have implications for conduct.

To educate the first, we can alter the cognition of objects; lions must be seen to be lazy as well as ferocious. In this way we can learn to control the fear in the interests of rational flight. In this way, too, we can overcome colour prejudices of repugnance by a fuller and more accurate cognizance of the object. And so there would be a chance that we would not shrink from coloured people so easily, once we come to know them more fully.

For, of course, it *is* important to distinguish between different ways in which emotion can conceive objects. I may show anger and kick the cat because it is a nasty, mean animal which, given half a chance, will scratch the baby, and has just spoilt my favourite flower bed; or I may kick it because I have just had a row with my wife and the cat is a substitute on which I can vent my spleen. The cat, in some sense, is an object of my wrath. But, in the one case, my emotion (given that babies and even flower beds are valuable) is evoked by a hateful object and my way of conceiving the world is appropriate, in some degree; in the other, my outbreak simply signalizes an internal disorder and in no way leads me to conceive the object aright.

Emotions, then, may even here manifest themselves in right or wrong conduct; they are not necessarily symptoms of disorder, though they may be. Whether they are or not is closely bound up with the correct cognition of the object, and in order to educate our emotions in the sense that we make them more appropriate to the object we need to know more about the world.

But then it is arguable that even if the cat is hateful and treacherous kicking it, if not altogether an unwarranted response, is, in fact, rather a crude way of dealing with the situation. It shows a certain lack of compassion for *la condition féline*. How do you foster feelings which go beyond (in the sense that they are ethically better) a more immediate, if partly justifiable, response to the object? In what sense, for instance, can we speak of refining the emotions?

In trying to answer the first question, it seems to me, we can learn from the Macbeth example. Given the context of personal ambition and egotistical desires in terms of which Macbeth obviously, from many evidences in the play, existed, his understanding of the object—in this case the king—was not an unjust one, nor his plan to murder Duncan unjustifiable; given the premises, the object was rightly conceived of as a stumbling block which must be removed if desires were to flourish. What then made Macbeth hesitate?—a pattern of feelings and emotions symbolized in such key-concepts as 'host', 'virtues', 'pity', 'cherubim'. His hysteria reveals aspects of the situation which are hidden both to the desiring and the calculating self, as I have suggested. From this it follows that emotions can be both informative and have implications which are ethical; if they are disturbances, they can disturb for the good of the person. They are not simply symptoms of disorder to be kept under control by the reason; they may, indeed, reveal truths beyond the reach of reason in the sense, at least, of calculating rationality. Virtue here involves giving way to one's emotions, releasing the element of control. Like acts of conation and cognition, states of emotion are ethically distinguishable; and, insofar as emotions as feelings may also involve emotions as motives, the ethical implications of states of feeling are of considerable importance.

Education, here, then, involves encouraging the 'healthy',

the ethically desirable, states of feeling in the sense that what they are about is truly revelatory about the world. This means that we must accept the emotions as possible modes of awareness which can *reveal, not simply recognise*, something about the world. What they reveal is often capable, as a result of human development, of articulation into a 'language', a commonly accepted set of symbols and significances which may have the power to define and hence to re-evoke the emotion concerned—even when 'recollected in tranquillity'. Fortunately, over the centuries, bodies of work involving different sorts of accepted symbolization have been built up in myth, literature and a variety of arts. My point is that such bodies of work should be treated with a seriousness equal to that with which we treat the disciplines relevant to cognition. We are always being told that the function of our education is to make children think. If my argument here has been correct, it is equally necessary to teach children how to feel; for some such feelings are as important a way of taking the world, as apprehensive of aspects of reality, as are our cognitions. In this sense at least they can become ethically desirable.

But we may find one manifestation of emotion more 'refined' than another, even when both are ethically acceptable. We need, then, to ask in what sense we can speak of refinement of emotion. It is part of the argument of this essay that emotion can become manifest through a complex articulation of feeling, cognition, perhaps action, perhaps speech. Sensation is usually an important element in any state of emotion to which human beings are subject, but this sensation may appear in more or less sophisticated forms. It may manifest itself in butterflies in the stomach, or in grunts or groans. But grunts or groans, for instance, may emerge as pure sounds of despair or despondency or become translated into complex structures of sound which have some cognitive as well as affective content.[1] (This, of

[1] That is to say, in accordance with what we discussed earlier, cognitive elements employed emotively. Those who are concerned to preserve the primacy of cognition sometimes argue that this constitutes cognition 'coloured' by emotion. But why should it not be regarded as emotion 'coloured' by cognitive elements?

course, is what happens in the latter part of the Macbeth speech.) Again, it must be remembered that not all joys are the same joy, nor all fears the same fear. There is the fear of lions; and there is the fear of being afraid of lions. The former could be described as the cruder fear in the sense, at least, that it could provide motive for an ethically less developed standard of behaviour. In the one case, we run away and leave the girl friend to the mercy of claws and jaw; in the other we stand firm. We are silly to fear spiders of the non-poisonous variety, but right to fear God.

Once this is admitted, we come to distinguish between emotions to which we apply the same generic term. But even when it *seems* to be the same fear, or joy or hate or discontent, it can manifest itself in less or more refined ways; and in doing so it does, in some degree, become a subtly different emotion. The baby, when it is hungry, sets up a great yell of anger at the neglect of its wants—a really quite appalling noise of deplorable crudity. Gradually these feelings come to be refined through a growing capacity for articulation through language. 'Want din-din' is a rather more refined expression of the yell, though lacking in the niceties of civilized intercourse. *Language in some at least of its uses involves such a refinement of primitive yells and cries, sighs and groans.*[1] 'My heart aches . . .' replaces, in part, a great sigh as a manifestation of regret and despair. It goes beyond the sigh because it contains not only the sigh but an awareness of aspects of sighing; *but it does contain the sigh*, the sigh is an *essential* part of the awareness. The awareness defines the exact nature of the sigh—it is this *sort* of sigh. But it is also this sort of *sigh*.

---

[1] It may be argued that yells of hate and sighs of grief are only *symptoms* of emotion, not the emotions themselves. But the word 'symptom' introduces a false dichotomy into the situation. A 'symptom' is simply an outward manifestation serving the purpose of recognition: sneezes and running noses are symptoms of a bad cold—but they also *are* the cold, or part of that complex of morbidity which we term a cold. It would be odd to say, 'He has a running nose and a cold'. In the same way, yells and sighs are symptoms of an emotion—but they are the emotion or part of that complex of psychic movement we call an emotion. It would be odd to say, 'He spoke heatedly and was angry'. The same would be true if we substituted 'expression' for 'symptom'.

The Education of the Emotions

In some sense, then, we can say that the first few lines of Keats's *Ode* represent a refined version of a sigh. What, then, constitutes refinement in *this* context? What the poem does is to avoid the vagueness, the indeterminate quality of the sigh with its hint of undifferentiated grief, and yet the sense of aching drowsiness is still *felt*. The sigh, in fact, is refined into a particular sort of sigh—it is made a precise sigh: this is not a contented sigh or just a tired sigh, but a sigh arising out of a particular sort of *weltsmerz*. Human development proceeds, in part at least, out of an ability to make finer and finer discriminations. Even to primitive man, presumably, not all sighs were the same sigh— but he lacked the discriminatory finesse and the linguistic development to enable him to define, to articulate distinctions among similarly named emotional states. The emotion remains an emotion—but it becomes a much more *precise* emotion through this sort of definition, distinguishable from all the other sorts of feelings expressed by sighs one could experience.

In thus articulating a precise sort of sigh one has *refined* one's feelings because one has distinguished between analogous, but different feelings related to different complexes of affectivity. In this developing self-consciousness, distinguishing between different sighs and fears and fears of fears, one is surely refining aspects of the inner life, developing consciousness, enabling one to become involved in a much wider range of affective experiences. At the same time, we may be said to be educating the emotions in that we are enabling people to feel the emotion relevant to *this* more sophisticated sort of sigh rather than to a cruder sort—for the *feeling* implicit in sighs is surely of many different kinds; and the feeling itself is in more degree controlled by the expression. Is it not true, indeed, that certain *forms* of expression may operate, as part of their function, in helping to contain emotion? If we are angry but express it in terms of 'Please be quiet' rather than 'Shut up', does not the former help us to contain our anger (and hence make it at least a different degree of anger) whereas the latter does not? Are not the precise nature of the feelings themselves bound up with the forms of expression? And will not hearing

F   81

The Education of the Emotions

the latter rather than the former in itself help to stimulate what in many circumstances will appear to be a coarser emotional response? The forms of human expression play their part in the education of the emotions. If we bear this in mind then, can we not also develop *new* sorts of feeling—or, at least, more refined versions of feelings we already have?

This raises the question, then, as to whether we can *teach* children how to feel? We can, at least as successfully as we can teach them how to think—which implies the possibility of deficiency in both spheres: the psychopath suffers from a form of feeling-deficiency equivalent to that suffered in the mental sphere by the mentally defective child. For one thing, we can ourselves set children an example of right feeling behaviour; we can avoid kicking the cat even when it is rather a nasty brute. A good deal of the talk about pupil-teacher relationships carries rather a sickly air with it. But it is praiseworthy in so far as it demonstrates right feelings—and such feelings would avoid a sickly pandering, would reveal value and emphasis, would suffuse the important with affect and, above all, avoid sentimentality: anger has a place when the object is anger-worthy.

Furthermore, we can employ rhetorics which are revelatory of feelings and of the resolutions of conflicts of feelings. If emotions can become manifest through articulation in a given rhetoric, as I have argued, is there not a chance that prolonged involvement in the refined rhetorics of others—perhaps through dramatic or mimetic representation—helps to build up structures of feeling educative to the total personality? As D. H. Lawrence appreciated, we learn how to feel much of what we come to feel through the persuasions and articulations of the rhetorics we encounter. Sighs, after all, are catching; so surely are the articulations of sighs. Affect is communicable. The emotions of children are, to some extent, plastic,[1] and they can, within limits, be helped to feel what we want them to feel through processes of involvement. It should be as important to

[1] Else how do we explain that passions which move some societies strongly, as that of romantic love (in the West) fail to appear in others, equally subject to sexual urges (cf. India, Africa, etc.).

The Education of the Emotions

protect them from examples of cheap feeling as it is to guard
them from examples of shoddy thinking. In so far as they become aware of the power of good images and rhythms, colours
and forms, sounds and movements through participation, to
that extent they have an opportunity to build up patterns of
affectivity which, as with Macbeth, stand them in good stead at
moments even of sharp crisis.

Hence there is a need for a great deal of involvement so
that a high degree of assimilation can take place of forms of
expression (linguistic, tactual, gestural, among others) which,
in their rhythms and movements exercise a delicately controlling *and* releasing effect. There is nothing particularly esoteric
about this notion; consider, for instance, the effects on our
behaviour of the different sorts of clothes we wear. Children
dressed up for a play will move and behave in ways quite
different from their normal selves; they may even speak differently. In the same way, differences in everyday clothes introduce subtle modifications of conduct; a young girl will
create a quite different form of behaviour in her party frock to
what she will in her jeans; the mini-skirt no doubt fosters a
different range of self-consciousness to that of the 'new look' in
the immediate post war years. In general we pay far too little
attention to the educative rôle of 'forms', sartorial, linguistic,
gestural and so on, though traditionally the educative rôle of
such forms has been long appreciated.

Three questions, perhaps, remain here, to be dealt with
briefly. Argument is subject to logical analysis, where the
rules are pretty clear and unequivocal—though not wholly so.
Are not these things I have referred to matters of taste, which
are notoriously arbitrary? But taste isn't arbitrary—it is subject
to refinement and training; and there are standards of taste
which can be argued about just as there are standards of logical
argument. Taste which has been genuinely disciplined leads to
no more—though no less—argument than do logical disputes
in the pages of the books of philosophers. Both will reveal
disagreement, but the level at which dispute occurs will be a
comparatively high one in both cases. No one who has had a

literary training will mistake Ian Fleming for an important writer, just as no one who has had a philosophical one will be likely to look to the leaders in the cheap press for flawless logic.

We need to bring children up to learn how to feel as well as how to behave and think? We do, indeed, and the three elements are more interconnected than we might imagine. It's a tough business, bringing up children.

But it didn't do Macbeth much good, did it? He still killed the king. True, but in doing so, he knew what he was doing. The choice was open to him and so he becomes a tragic, not a pathetic figure. At least in his wrong doing he was more fully human than the psychopath: and to achieve this is to achieve a sort of human dignity.

Finally, it must be said that the disorder view of emotion, the idea that it is something irrational which needs purging away, has too long a history to be summarily dismissed. Are there not, indeed, destructive impulses which need to be brought under rational control? Is not the attitude one takes up—emotion as leading to creative organization, emotion as leading to disorder, to destruction—partly a matter of what emotions are involved as well as a matter of two ethical ideals? Perhaps at the back of the one is an ideal of the intensification of life, and at the back of the other a transcendence of life.[1] But may not both have something to say relevant to our thinking about the emotions? There is the need both for the stable and the dynamic, for the purging of certain stresses as well as for the intensification and refinement of others. Some emotions, at least, are without positive value, constitute a defect, a madness; at the basis of their inadequacy lies their misconception of the object. Of this, my example above of kicking the cat as an outlet for my disatisfaction with my wife might constitute a trivial example; nevertheless, it indicates how emotion can serve the unrestrained, constitute an outpouring of venom which in no way adequately conceives the object. Here the therapy is largely

[1] 'There is developed a moral position against the desires and motions of the soul which are evidence of human imperfection and the Fall away from the divine order. Man, were he perfect, would need nothing, would desire nothing, and would have no emotion.' (Hillman: op.cit., p. 210.)

one of restraint or discharge, of treating such emotion as a disorder, of attempting to reassert an equilibrium, or of purging through release in socially approved ways. It is absurd to think that all emotion can be employed creatively, as a means of apprehending the world; and, indeed, in the past, certain rituals have explicitly had as their purpose release of tension. Their sole function has been that of the safety valve; they were socially approved ways, not of being more oneself, but of stopping being oneself. An example of this was the early Dionysiac ritual:

> If I understand Dionysiac ritual aright, its social function was essentially cathartic, in the psychological sense: it purged the individual of those infectious irrational impulses which, when damned up, had given rise, as they have done in other cultures, to outbreaks of dancing mania and similar manifestations of collective hysteria; it relieved them by providing them with a ritual outlet. . . . The joys of Dionysus had an extremely wide range, from the simple pleasures of the country bumpkin, dancing a jig on greased wineskins, to the ωμοφάγος χαρίς of the ecstatic bacchanal. At both levels, and at all levels between he is Lusios, 'the Liberator'—the god who by very simple means, or by other means not so simple, enables you for a short time to *stop being yourself*, and thereby sets you free. . . . As the Scythians in Herodotus put it, 'Dionysus leads people on to behave madly'—which could mean anything from 'letting yourself go' to becoming 'possessed'. The aim of his cult was *ecstasis*—which again could mean anything from 'taking you out of yourself' to a profound alteration of personality.[1]

Another way, of course, is through certain sorts of analysis and the 'transference' which results. But as I have made clear, this is not the business of education.[2]

We can sum up by saying that the concept 'emotion' relates to certain aspects of human behaviour of a more impulsive or energetic kind—the notion of movement is fundamental to its explanatory force. Such movement or motion constitutes a common factor underlying the various positive and negative emotions and may involve cognitive elements and behaviour of many different kinds. We may differ as to the extent to which

[1] E. R. Dodds: *The Greeks and the Irrational*, pp. 76–77.
[2] Cf. Chapters I and II.

The Education of the Emotions

we approve of these different manifestations of conduct; or we may differ as to whether we think people should be 'spontaneous' or 'impulsive' or otherwise 'emotional' at all. Our attitude to emotion, indeed, will depend a great deal on our conception of the ideal personality, and will, therefore, depend on prior value judgments concerning social behaviour and the sorts of people we admire. Hence two broad attitudes to emotion: one regards it as a disorder, because we appreciate calmness and rationality; the other regards it as a positive value because we admire warmth and 'feeling'. This corresponds to two broad ways of educating emotions: one leads to equilibrium by discharge, if necessary by therapeutic means, the other to reintegration at a higher, more 'refined' level where emotion will have a positive rôle to play, as a positive means of apprehending the world and therefore conducive to right conduct.

At least it is true that all people have emotions and, therefore, the question of coping with them (and educating them) is universal.

4

Myth and the School Child

The essential function of myth lies in the organization it affords to aspects of man's emotional life. It both gives expression to, and offers a framework for, some of his deepest hopes and fears. Originally it constituted an organ of reality rather than a mode of allegorical allusion; it did not, that is, refer to something which was thought to exist independently of itself, but was a means of grasping the thing-in-itself. Hence it represented one aspect of the human desire to live in an ordered world, to bring it under control by representation in symbolic *form*. It involved the projection of what was internal and subjective into objective and external modes, so that they could be shared communally and assimilated as manageable experience, albeit in vicarious guise. Closely connected with rite, myth expressed 'theoretically' what ritual communicated through behaviour and action. In both cases, a meaning was present which transcended surface implication. In the total pattern of man's attempts to cope with his world and find a place in which to be at home, myth fulfilled as important a function as that form of objectification which enabled him to cope with the practicalities of daily life and later came to be called science.

Furthermore, in the continuity of man's development, myth provided a powerful and essential element in his search for identity by affording a pedagogic image. 'It is not by its history that the mythology of a nation is determined', Cassirer has pointed out in his book, *The Myth of the State*, 'but, conversely, its history is determined by its mythology—or, rather, the mythology of a people does not *determine* but *is* its fate'. Men were inducted, through the power of their myths, into a variety of social forms of behaviour; for a mythology was peculiarly a characteristic of social life, *le désir collectif personifié*. Its heroes offered models for imitation, after the style of Homeric education, which appealed to myth as to a collection of authoritative instances. Plato saw thus the function of the poet in preserving the glory of the past in his poetry: 'Possession by the muses and their madness, invade a gentle and chaste soul, awaken it, and bewitch it with songs and all kinds of poesy; and by glorifying countless deeds of man of old, educate posterity.' Through seeking identification with the characters of the myths men could realize their own 'true' selves; for this involved a transcendence of their 'natural' selves. The *paradeigma*, the example for imitation, remained a fundamental concept of Greek education.

The decay of social forms in the modern world and the stress on personal individuality and 'naturalness' have destroyed the conscious and overt power of a central mythology to mould and structure behaviour; yet the influence of myth persists in more covert guise: 'when old, long-felt, self-coherent ways of life (rituals with their accompanying myths) are disrupted by 'modernism', most men (or all) are impoverished: as men can't live by abstractions alone, they have to fill their voids by crude extemporized, fragmentary myths (pictures of what might be or ought to be).[1] For men cannot build out of themselves their terms of existence, but must seek them in the images for conduct their social order presents. A 'much-divided civilization' offers, in the technical terminology of the sociologists, a variety of 'rôles'; in the language of the poet, a series of 'masks'. 'I think that all happiness depends on the energy to assume the mask of some other self', wrote W. B. Yeats, 'that all joyous or creative life is a re-birth of something not oneself, something which has no memory and is created in a moment and perpetually renewed'. Alas, the truth is more

[1] R. Wellek and A. Warren: *Theory of Literature*, p. 122.

Myth and the School Child

complex; for the joy derived is bound up with the adequacy of the rôles assumed; with Yeats it was usually that of the hero; but there are less inviting images for sale.

In fact, even the effort to be oneself raises inevitably the question: 'Which self?' For, given man's self-consciousness, the self must, in part, be the image of the self; and that image (or those images) derive to some extent from social experience. In so far as traditionally the great myths formed a crucial part of this social experience, enshrined in the memory of the race, the self image could achieve a high degree of qualitative consistency. Once the central myth is destroyed, though the great themes and problems of human identity—say of love or power—persist, social experience offers a less coherent, a more fragmented solution. It is open to the perversions of the marketplace. Myth can be created, as the dictators have shown—and as Plato recommended long ago. Vestiges of older myths, recast and often debased, continue to inform our social consciousness, and are expressed through various media of communication, and in a variety of fictional guises.

For, indeed, underlying the babel of rhetorics which now compete for assimilation, certain basic themes, traditionally structured by myth, persist. There is, for instance, the rôle of love (*agape* and *eros*) with which man has to come to terms— sex and other forms of love. M. Denis de Rougemont has traced the progress of the myth of romantic passion in his *Passion and Society*. Passion is itself only one possible cultural solution to the adjustment of relationships between the sexes, an adjustment which all societies must encompass; for such passion is foreign to the experience of many races. M. de Rougemont shows its origins in the West in the Tristan myth, through which passion was both stimulated *and contained*. In its original guise this myth brought to consciousness latent feelings and yet provided a framework within which these emotions could be rendered socially innocuous: 'If literature can be said to have affected the manners of Europe, the credit is certainly due to our myth. More accurately, it is due to the rhetoric of the myth, as inherited from Provençal love. . . . The adoption of certain linguistic conventions naturally involves and fosters the rise of the latent feelings most apt to be expressed in this way. That is the sense in which it may be said, following La Rochefoucauld, that few people would fall in love had they never heard of love. . . . The emotions first experienced by an upper class and then through imitation by the masses are literary creations in the sense that a given rhetoric is the sufficient condition for them to be avowed and hence for them to become conscious.'

From the stand-point of the educationist, the most interesting feature of de Rougemont's analysis lies in its demonstration of the '*power which (the myth) gains over us, usually without our knowing it*'. For this indicates the pedagogic force of the culture, even in its forms of literary and, therefore, vicarious expression. Furthermore, his analysis indicates the crucial nature of the particular *form* taken by the mythical expression. Originally, the achievement of the Tristan myth had been to 'enclose passion in a framework, to bring its unruly surge within the restraint of a set of conventions'; it had served to restrain the lawlessness of passion (while in part creating what it sought to contain) and to fit it into moral categories. But now 'all young people breathe in from books and periodicals, from stage and screen, and from a thousand daily allusions, a romantic atmosphere in the haze of which passion seems to be the supreme test that one day or another awaits every true man or woman, and it is accepted that nobody has ever really lived till he or she "has been through it" '. The myth is now one of boundless aspiration, it has been vulgarized and appears in a variety of tawdry guises.

It can manifest itself, for instance, as something one owes oneself, quite apart from any genuine mutuality or reciprocity. As the centrally embracing myths of a society fragment, a multiplicity of identities is offered for assimilation on a personal rather than a communal basis. This is at once a sign of and a means of implementing a greater degree of social fluidity, when the traitional barriers no longer act as a check to ambition. A brilliant analysis of the *prestige* of passion, imbibed vicariously from reading and closely associated with status aspirations in an increasingly mobile society, is to be found in Stendhal's *Le Rouge et le Noir*. Here is demonstrated the 'education' (Stendhal himself uses the word) afforded by vicarious experience in a society of shifting boundaries, such as we have come increasingly to inhabit; and Stendhal shows himself sensitive to the formative rôle played by the 'mythology' of passion, as set forth in memoirs and works of literature, in stimulating its incidence. Here passion is represented as part of the self-regarding *persona* rather than something evoked by the other person: it arises out of a silent dialogue between original endowment and vicarious experience. It provides us with an admirable example of the persistent power of myth to shape personality and action; and yet it shows itself in a sadly perverted form for now it encourages indulgence rather than containment.

Fundamentally, perhaps, Julien Sorel is moved by notions of his own social inferiority; the novel is certainly one about class. He has great pride; the image in terms of which he seeks to form himself is that of Napoleon; his favourite book—he is introduced to us as a reader—is the *Mémorial de Sainte-Hélène*. His outlook on society has been formed by Rousseau's *Confessions*. His third love is a collection of Bulletins of the *Grande Armée*. Other books he looks on as 'so many lying documents, written by fraudulent knaves for their own advancement'; but he read many. And he dreams—of success; when the red (the army) no longer offers itself as a possible means, he seeks the black (the priesthood). Even the title of the book cunningly suggests that this young man will adopt the outward style and garb which will best serve his secret ambitions. He possesses in himself no independent being or integrity; he seeks simply success in the terms which certain current formulations offer; he sees in such success a mark of superiority in a society of mediocrity which constitutes the 'reality' by which he is surrounded. He sees love, primarily at least, not as a mutual relationship, but as something he *owes* himself, in the delineation of the image he has chosen for himself:

> From his earliest childhood, he had experienced moments of ecstatic excitement. Then it was that he revelled in dreams of

being one day introduced to beautiful Parisian women, whose attention he could manage to attract by some remarkable feat or other. Why should he not be loved by one of them, just as Bonaparte, when still poor, had been loved by that distinguished lady, Madame de Beauharnais? For many years past Julien had not let, perhaps, a single hour go by without telling himself that Bonaparte, an unknown, penniless lieutenant, had made himself master of the world with his sword.[1]

We learn, then, from the models our writers have formed for us. In so far as they participate in the longings and hopes, fears and aspirations of their generation they articulate and make conscious for the community of the literate feelings and desires which define areas of understanding formerly the province of traditional myth and legend. This, indeed, has been half-consciously their aim once, with the coming of the romantics, literature has ceased to be an adornment and has come to realize, obscurely, its power. Such explorations of experience, of course, reveal some differences from traditional myth-making. They are written, not oral; they are more indirectly communal, though they belong to the community of the literate; their influence remains pedagogic but more indirectly so—to be caught rather than taught perhaps. But they share with myth its affective power; they involve the externalization of inner desires and fears into symbolic forms which necessitate fiction as a means of transmitting a reality.

Rousseau himself was aware of the effect literature had had on him; and Stendhal's novel is in itself a tribute to the image-forming and conduct-directing power of the written word in an age of developing literacy—and, in this case, of its power of corruption. For Julien Sorel, the women he seeks are primarily symbols of a success he craves. He represents the search for a mode of self-assertion in a society increasingly anti-heroic and bourgeois. And, indeed, this young man, though he displays some heroic qualities, is forced to conduct his campaigns in terms which appear comparatively petty; the conquests he makes are those of women's hearts, the only shots he fires

[1] The translation used is that by M.R.B. Shaw and published by Penguin.

Myth and the School Child

characteristically miss or wound only superficially. Furthermore, he mistakes his own nature; only when he abandons his pretensions does he assume the true rôle of lover.

In a period of social vulgarity or inadequacy men of imagination are likely all the more strongly to seek models where they can find them—and where more likely than in the imaginative works of the epoch? In this way, Julien Sorel is a historically significant figure; not that this sort of thing could not have happened before[1], but that people were coming to be self-conscious about its happening and to see it as part of the life they depict. Sorel stands at a particular point in the development of self-consciousness, and at a particular stage of social evolution. It is peculiarly significant, for instance, that much of the later action takes place in a library—the repository of historical aspirations.

Sorel comes to see his conquest of Madame de Rênal, then, as part of a plan of campaign of personal assertion. In the midst of his unself-conscious delight in the life he is leading with the de Rênal's, he happens, one evening, to touch Madame de Rênal's hand:

> This hand was very quickly withdrawn; but Julien felt it his *duty* to manage things so that this hand should not be withdrawn when he touched it. The idea of a duty to be carried out, and of making himself ridiculous or rather being made to feel his inferiority if he failed, banished at once every thought of pleasure from his heart (p. 70).

He is both inside and outside his 'myth'; he doesn't *live* it unself-consciously, but it affects him deeply. What was once an organ of reality has now become one among other *images* of reality; but reality it remains, in so far as it structures his hopes and aspirations, formulates the stress and emphasis of his emotional life. This is the young man who has derived what ideas he has about women from

> Certain of Napoleon's remarks about women, together with one or two of his disquisitions on the merits of novels fashionable in his reign ... (p. 69).

[1] It happens in *Don Quixote*, earlier—and in *Madame Bovary*, later.

What is involved is purely prestige, the will to conquer, with no hint of tenderness; when the hand becomes his, Sorel is happy,

> not from any love for Madame de Rênal, but because a frightful state of torment was at an end (p. 72).

His demands on his employer he conceives in terms of Napoleonic campaigns. He has been reading 'his favourite book':

> Soon, however, he put down his book. Reflecting on Napoleon's victories had made him aware of some new feature in his own. Yes, he said to himself, I've won a battle. I must press home my advantage; I must crush the pride of this arrogant gentleman while he's in retreat. That's true Napoleonic strategy. I must ask for three days' holiday to go and see my friend Fouqué. If he refuses, I'll take a high hand with him, and he'll give in (p. 84).

The pettiness of the victory—in what terms can a request for three days' leave be compared to a Napoleonic victory?—throws an ironic light both on Julien and on the society in which only such victories are possible. Always he needs to live up to his own *self*-image; the influence of any communal view is no longer sufficiently potent: 'I owe it to myself all the more to succeed with this woman', he thinks, on another occasion. And the basic fault, interestingly enough, is put down to education, as if there was a conflict between the 'easy nonchalance' of true rôle assumption and the self images fostered by the instruction of a complex civilization:[1]

> Such, alas! is the result of over-civilization. At twenty, a young man's heart, provided he has had a little education, is a thousand

[1] To my mind, Stendhal here misrepresents the complexity of the issues raised. In his reference to 'easy nonchalance', and in the outcome of the novel, Stendhal seems to be exploiting a common theme of romantic writings, the conflict of 'naturalness' and 'artificiality'. If only Julien had been content with the offerings of 'easy nonchalance', he could have happily enjoyed Mme de Rênal: 'In the past, when I might have been so happy during our walks in the woods of Vergy, my fiery ambition carried my mind away into imaginary countries', he says to Mme de Rênal before he dies. But Mme de Rênal was a married woman, so that an 'easy nonchalance' was hardly an appropriate attitude to the network of duties and obligations implicit in her married state. There is not much in the moral order that can be achieved by 'natural' man, enmeshed as he inevitably is in the network of his culture; but he can pursue better or worse images of conduct; and he can be sustained in the pursuit of the better by the pedagogic power of great myth.

miles away from that easy nonchalance without which love is often nothing but the most tedious of duties (p. 96).

The effect of this is to spoil the delights he is offered, though, at the same time, it is also a mark of his superiority; because, in a sense, the image he pursues represents something superior to the banality of the society he inhabits:

> Yet, even at the most sweetly blissful moments a victim of his own queer pride, he still aspired to play the part of a man accustomed to subduing women to his will, and made incredibly determined efforts to spoil what was lovable in himself. When he might have been attentive to the transports he aroused, and the remorse that only served to heighten their eager ecstasy, he kept the idea of a *duty to himself* unceasingly before his eyes. He was afraid of feeling terrible regret and of making himself for ever ridiculous if he departed from the model of perfection he had resolved to follow. In a word, what made Julien a superior being was the very thing that prevented him from enjoying this happiness right in front of his eyes. He was like a sixteen-year-old girl with charming colouring who is silly enough to put on rouge when going to a ball.

So, where his affair with Madame de Rênal is concerned, passion for Julien, at least in its earlier stages, is another name for ambition—the ambition of the *étranger* whose images of success and glory exist essentially in terms of his *reading*. Much the same is true of his relationship with Mathilde—except that here, both parties are affected by the mythologies they have absorbed. Mathilde is as much under the sway of certain aspects of the history of her house—and of the sensibility she has derived from novels—as Julien is under that of Napoleon. When, for instance, she begins to suspect she is in love with Julien, it is to romantic models she goes for confirmation:

> She ran over in her mind all the descriptions of passion she had read in *Manon Lescaut*, the *Nouvelle Héloïse*, the *Lettres d'une Réligieuse Portugaise*, and so forth. There was no question, of course, of anything but a *grande passion*; a trivial love affair would have been unworthy of a girl of her age and birth. She gave the name of love only to that heroic feeling which was to be met with in France in the days of Henri III and Bassompierre. A

love of this sort never basely succumbed to obstacles; far from that, it made one do great deeds. What a misfortune for me, she thought, that there's no real Court like that of Catherine de Medici or Louis XIII. I feel myself equal to everything that is most daring and most great. What couldn't I do with a king who was a man of spirit, like Louis XIII, sighing at my feet! I'd lead him into the Vendée, as Baron de Tolly so frequently remarks, and from there he'd win back his kingdom; then there'd be an end to the Charter . . . and Julien would help me. What's lacking in him? Name and fortune. He'd make a name for himself, he'd acquire a fortune (p. 321).

And she, too, has an image of the type of love affair she owes herself. When the two come together in a scene of considerable psychological complexity—for it is the meeting of two people who are so much bound up with self-images that they both fail to achieve any real level of reciprocity, and Julien is reduced to quoting phrases from the *Nouvelle Héloïse* in order to cope with the situation—it is rightly considered that

> Passionate love was still rather more of a model they were imitating than the real thing (p. 352).

And, in reality, the novels let them down:

> There was nothing unforeseen for her in all the events of that night except the unhappiness and the shame she had experienced in place of the perfect bliss of which the novels tell us (p. 353).

Julien is elated—but only with a conquest, not with love.

Julien, indeed, feels as a 'young Second Lieutenant, who as a result of some astonishing exploit has just been made a Colonel, on the field, by his Commander in Chief' (p. 353). Mathilde, in her love, must always, because of her pride, 'include the idea of an audience' (p. 472); what she wants is the sort of love which belongs to past heroic times—love of a kind that 'made hearts beat in the age of Charles IX and Henri III' (p. 473). Her carrying Julien's head on her knee to the funeral remains entirely typical of her self-dramatization and her sense of the romantic. She satisfies her 'longing to astonish the world by the extravagance of her love and the sublimity of her ventures'.

Myth and the School Child

Here, then, we have a novel which, in its probing, as all great literature probes, reveals the extent to which the realities we inhabit are themselves in part the creation of the books we have read, of the mythical formulations we have encountered, and which become part of our own self-creation. The novel betokens the coming to prominence of classes hitherto submerged, who by right of birth have played only a lowly part on the world's stage, and the degradation of an aristocracy which has been shorn of its ability to *act*. The effect on superior minds in both classes is to make them wish to achieve the prominence, to taste the personal self-satisfactions implicit in the fantasies of power and effectiveness they have absorbed from their reading.

For, it has been said, 'true myth presents its images and its imaginary actors, not with the playfulness of fantasy, but with a compelling authority'. But, how can fantasy remain playful when the compulsions of traditional myth have eroded away under the influence of a rational scepticism. Does not then 'playful fantasy', in the resulting vacuum, come itself to assume something of a pedagogic rôle, take on the guise traditionally assumed by that profounder form of fantasy, myth? Is there not more than a modicum of truth in the romantic poet's assumption of the rôle of 'unacknowledged legislator'? And is any fantasy now so 'playful'—in an era that has, indeed, learnt to take play seriously—that it may not contain a threat to someone's integrity, not provide a doubtful rôle or a mask that someone will adopt? And is not the nature of that rôle or mask in need of ethical discrimination—to reveal the adequacy of the rôles which are offered?

II

It is because of a suspicion that the answer to such questions would provide a jolt to complacency that we come to realize the need to scrutinize closely the rhetorics of popular culture which our children encounter; for, if my analysis so far has been correct, they contain within themselves considerable power to shape and organize. All young people growing up need sustaining in their search for identity; for 'identity' in growth is a fluid entity, and, we have come to suspect from the foregoing analysis, much subject to the vagaries of the particular images for conduct to which it attaches itself. At the heart of current cultural experience, for instance, lies a conflict of ethics; there is the older, traditional ethic based on the notion of self-transcendence, so that 'being' is ever subordinate to 'becoming', in a search for a higher 'form'; and there is that based on current self projection, when 'becoming' only seems to be made up of more of present 'being' and the evanescent impulses that inform it.[1]

Now, there is a part of young people that desperately wants to 'become', to adapt—at least—to current forms as they sense these are recognized by the adult world. The thirteen year old secondary modern schoolgirl who wrote: 'I don't think that people would think much of you if you went into a big posh hotel or restaurant and asked for fish and chips or something like that. I think you should take the class of the restaurant and then order something which you think suits that type of restaurant',[2] was rather touchingly trying to find her way about amidst the social complexities of the adult world. In its very limited and trivial way her anxiety was expressed in her desire to abide by the current conventions of different social atmospheres; and her worries are what, when she is a little older, the advertisers will exploit at about that level of triviality. For what she is seeking is not true maturity but the external trappings and privileges of growing up—though she is not yet in a position to recognize the difference. Thus, when the sixth form college is supported on the grounds that it will allow young people to be treated in a more adult manner, what is often meant by this is the provision of coffee bars, freedom to smoke and to use lipstick and to adopt other of the superficial privileges of adulthood. These are

[1] Or the opposition can be put in terms of 'puritan' and 'fun' morality: cf. Wolfenstein, 'Fun Morality: An Analysis of Recent American Child-training Literature' reprinted in M. Mead and M. Wolfenstein (ed.) *Childhood in Contemporary Cultures*.
[2] A Loughborough school girl.

Myth and the School Child

symbols of manliness and womanhood the advertisers feed on—and, indeed, stimulate a desire for. These are the myths of growing up implicit in modern commercialism.

At the same time, she will encounter a contemporary youth sub-culture one strand of which may well stress the opposing virtues of, in some sense, 'being herself', implying her 'natural' self. This sounds attractive; it ties in with an important strand of romantic thought which has exercised its influence since the late eighteenth century threw off the conventions of an aristocratic society. In fact, in most of its guises, the ideal is a false one, for the 'true' self only emerges as a result of a profound effort of self discovery; it is an offshoot of wisdom and the acquiring of restraints, not the surrender to impulse it so often pretends to be. And, indeed, our schoolgirl will not be encouraged to acquire this wisdom but will be inducted by her youth culture into the pursuit of what it *teaches* her to consider her 'true' self. In the midst of her uncertainties, it will encourage her to react against the necessary restraints of really growing up, in precisely the same way that she has been encouraged to throw over the restraints of childhood to which I referred in the last paragraph. In both cases it is restraints that suffer and unmodified desires that gain. Now, however, she will be encouraged to shudder away from the world of the 'squares', of the 'phonies' (Holden Caulfield's word in Salinger's *Catcher in the Rye*) in the name of 'being honest with herself', of 'sincerity'. Most young people today, if they knew of it, would react violently against the 'artificiality' implicit in Yeats's doctrine of the masks. This they would see as the supreme manifestation of adult phoniness. Today, their 'heroism' is that of the anti-heroic, of the formless and the 'natural'; they fail to see that this encourages its own sort of 'phoniness'.

Here I must break off to meet two possible objections. It will be urged, in the first place, that there are no sufficiently defined ways of behaviour and values among young people to warrent the attribution to them of a youth sub-culture. This has been argued recently by Dr. Marie Jahoda and Mr. Neil Warren in a review article devoted to some of the relevant literature.[1] Their point is that research material demonstrates both continuities and discontinuities between young people and the adult world, and that it is a matter of choice which is emphasized.

Now it is perfectly true that the lines of demarcation with the adult world are in no way rigid. For one thing, as I shall point out later, adults themselves participate in the rituals of adolescence and rather pathetically try to 'live it up' with their children—they become 'pals'.[2] Young people, too, participate in some forms of adult activities, some doing so much more than others. Nevertheless, the enormously increased spending power of young people has made them into a recognizable 'market' for fashions, 'pop' idols and other commodities and has, therefore, helped to create a way of living with recognizable features, if only as an abstraction from and an accentuation of certain adult trends. In so far as one needs to work in terms of one model rather than another it is reasonable to assume the presence rather than the absence of identifiable modes of behaviour characteristic of at least important sections of young people. The fact that so few have family responsibilities as compared with the adult world, inevitably involves different patterns of behaviour and different opportunities. Without putting into the notion more than it can bear, then, I must accept the idea of a recognizable youth sub-culture—if only as a manifestation of intensity. After all, who else *screams* for the Beatles?

But then it will also be urged that much evidence points to a high degree of conformity among young people to parental standards: 'The influence of parents on the standards, values and behaviour of their children (even in their teens) is, in general, supreme', writes Professor Musgrove in his recent

---

[1] *Sociology of Education*, Winter, 1965.

[2] This, of course, is very much of an American phenomenon. This is partly because, 'In America we regard childhood as a very nearly ideal time, a time for enjoyment, an end in itself.' This contrasts with French attitudes, where the main effort is to grow up and childhood is looked on as a period of probation. Cf 'French Parents take their children to the Park' by Martha Wolfenstein, reprinted in *Childhood in Contemporary Cultures* ed. Mead and Wolfenstein. American influences, of course, are spreading.

Myth and the School Child

The Family, Education and Society. And he produces a good deal of evidence from a variety of sources to back it up. Nevertheless, there are modifications to his thesis to be made. For one thing, that aspect of personality orientation affected by the fragmentary myths of our time is the most difficult to investigate; what emerges to the social science researcher is usually the rational answer to the rational mode of investigation. Even with refined techniques it is too much to expect young people to reveal their lusts, dreams and aspirations, their areas of discontent—other than as a general irritability, the effects on their exposed raw nerves of growing up—other than as a pervasive lack of communication, an obstinate silence in the face of questionings. Can we expect them to reveal the images they pursue in their first tentative approaches to the opposite sex? Yet it is often in the field of sex relationships that they need most help. We must go on hints and clues, the insights of great artists like Stendhal and extrapolations from the culture that appeals, the forms that involve and manifest themselves, if only fleetingly, in dress and behaviour. 'Nothing in this world seems to live up to my best fantasies', says Morgan in the film of that name; *his* Napoleon turns out to be Tarzan. When these are the themes and explorations of popular art, the ability of the audience to recognize in them its own image seems assured. The implication is that even the common man recognizes himself in Walter Mitty or Billy Liar. The Sorel syndrome has attacked the masses; and it will, in general, bite at the moment of deepest uncertainty —adolescence, though most profoundly, perhaps, with the unusual and imaginative child.[1]

[1] It is interesting to note that both Walter Mitty and Billy Liar assume multiple personalities rather than a single one, as in the case of Sorel. This is an indication of the ubiquity of rôle assumption, as a manifestation of the sheer volume of offered images. In general we need to know much more about how young people, at various times and in various situations, see themselves. What images are pursued by the ton-up kids, the mods and rockers, the prize winners and school captains in the achievement of their chosen pursuits, and how do they make their choices among the conflicting rôles their culture offers them? For 'drives' and aspirations often participate in a motion-picture on the screens of memory. In conducting research at this highly complex and delicate level the novelist provides us with a useful model. (Cf. my *Education and Values*, pp. 162–3.) We can use it to under-

Myth and the School Child

As one aspect of this syndrome, then, the young, I have said, will pursue their version of the 'natural'. Yet underlying their cult of 'sincerity' as an intended reaction against adult forms and stuffiness is simply a conventional acceptance of their own notions of 'reality'. For, ironically enough, the basic premises of their own conventions of honesty and formlessness are derived from the psychological reductionism which has been one characteristic of the post-Freudian adult world. Such reductionism has encouraged an acceptance of the more primitive and elemental expressions of human drives as in some way 'truer' than long evolved social conventions. Naturally, this has chimed in well with the unformed quality of youth, and has provided an ethic which militates against growing up. In actual fact, the acceptance of this ethic is simply an indication of the retreat from the alternative ethic of self transcendence, with its reliance on mature social forms for its implementation. And this retreat has been much assisted—in fact, in part, created—by the literary attack on the forms of social behaviour which has characterized so much the rhetoric of modern writings. The decay of style and form in behaviour and relationship is not the least of the charges to be laid against the minor writers of the twentieth century.[1]

For, to find the world of adult forms just 'phoney', as does Salinger's character, in *Catcher in the Rye*, is in part to *create* the vacuum which it is thought is being revealed. As Professor Erich Heller points out in a recent essay on Nietzsche, 'there are secrets which are *created* in the process of their revelation'; and he quotes Nietzsche, that 'it is the sign of a finer humanity to respect "the mask" and not, in the wrong places, indulge in psychology and psychological curiosity'; he glosses this by urging that 'He who does not *wish* to see what is great

stand the ways in which young people come to explore new emotional territory: 'She is all States and all Princes I' . . . does not the metaphor *structure* the relationship, as the man sees it?

[1] Professor Jules Henry gives a biting analysis of 'the anomic acquaintanceship', 'the erosion of preface' and 'the purple vistas of impulse release' which characterise aspects of teen-age relationships in his excellent *Culture against Men*, which only came to hand after this essay was written.

Myth and the School Child

in a man, has the sharpest eye for that which is low and superficial in him, and so gives away—himself.' As Professor Heller points out, 'When Hamlet has come to know the frailty of woman, he knows Ophelia not better than when he was 'unknowingly' in love with her; he only knows her differently and he knows her worse.' (*The Artist's Journey into the Interior*, p. 186.)

Such reductionism has encouraged the cult of the child, which is itself part of twentieth-century mythology. It is as if the unformed social world of the child was thought to constitute a superior form of social organization to that of the 'phoney' adult community. That children have a keen eye for some of the less attractive adult masks is a fair point; that they are capable of seeing the relevance to desirable social behaviour of certain other of these masks, or of understanding the greater social richness such forms introduce into our lives, would be to expect them to become what, in fact, they are not, that is, adult and not children. Yet the point can be illustrated in the simplest of ways. Some parents adopt the convention of allowing their children to call them by their Christian names. It seems more 'sincere' to do so. By encouraging this, however, they destroy a richness by denying to their children the experience of having, quite explicitly, a Father and a Mother; for the use of such terms involves rich affective overtones, which are bound up with their employment and which must necessarily be absent in the use of Christian names, a convention which reduces parents to the level of contemporaries, and diminishes the dimension of the relationship. For it also disparages the status of the child as son or daughter rather than merely friend. What one calls a person inevitably introduces a relevant 'tone' into the relationship.[1]

To assume, then, the 'mask' of Father or Mother is enriching

---

[1] The implication, as in other contexts where Christian names are now used inappropriately, is that such usage will contribute to 'right relationship'. What is forgotten is that relationships are of many different kinds, that each contributes its characteristic 'tone' and that each requires an appropriate form of address, not one that homogenizes all relationships to the pattern of close friendship. For then, what does one call one's real friends?

to the lives of children, however much at times they may want to reduce their parents to the level of 'Tom' or 'Lizzie'. By such devices is the affective life more richly structured; and such realizations must make us look with the keenest apprehension at the rhetorics—their form of expression, their adjustments of relationship, the underlying myths that inform them—by which our children are surrounded. For, all too often they exploit immaturity, a 'nudity' of personality, as if it was the greatest of virtues.

It is interesting, in this respect, to note that the emergence of a youth culture with some degree of autonomy from that of the adult world—constituting in part a repudiation of that world—necessitates a serious break with the traditional conventions concerning the rôle of adolescence and of the long continued seriousness with which the young have been initiated into the adult world, as a *rite de passage*. The function of this particular rite in primitive societies was to induct the growing child into his adult rôle, into becoming part of the adult world. Often it involved practices of considerable severity. It was usually conducted by strangers, in contrast to the more informal education of family and neighbours the child had so far undergone. In some cases (though not all) it could be of a severity likely to have consequences which could only be regarded as traumatic. The rituals were of a meticulously patterned character, and there was only one way of doing them: 'Every line painted on a boy's body, every movement of a performer, every word or phrase uttered, the right person to make every move, is rigidly prescribed as having to be done in one way only—the right way.' But, above all, the aim was cultural, not vocational. The initiate was taught the ceremonies and myths of the tribe. 'It is through the rigidly disciplined instruction of a common and rigidly prescribed curriculum that he assumes, with all his fellow tribesmen, a common culture.'[1] The adult world imposed itself without apology and without concession.

Such rites of initiation were part of a large corpus of cere-

[1] C. W. M. Hart: 'Contrasts between Prepubertal and Postpubertal Education', reprinted in *Education and Culture*, ed. G. D. Spendler, p. 415.

Myth and the School Child

monial, the chief feature of which was to bring home both the privileges and responsibilities of office, whether that of adulthood or of some more specific post or function. The rites normally imposed forcefully and vividly 'distinctive imperatives of apparel, speech, conduct and observance'; they were a means of inducting the initiate into a moral order: 'The actor, docile though he may be while undergoing the process of being incorporated, lives and acts the part once he possesses it. He appropriates this part to himself, he knows it, he has a commitment to it. It is through the acting of his part in accordance with the norms and sanctions that legitimize it that he is incorporated in the social structure. . . . He is made to appropriate his part to himself because it is in a sense outside himself.'[1] In such ways did the youth of yesteryear internalize the *mores* of the adult social structure and accept its responsibilities.

Vestiges of such rites persist into later times. Thus Father Ong writes of 'Latin Language Study as a Renaissance Puberty Rite', in which he finds analogies between the severity, the segregation, and the break with the informality of domestic ways which characterized primitive initiation, and the form and matter of the Latin schools of the Renaissance, where the boys were toughened by severity, initiated into the epic virtues of courage, and introduced into an extra-familial society. The progress of humanitarian sentiment has, of course, softened the procedures used in our schools today out of all recognition; but one cannot help sensing that other factors have entered into the transformation—and, in doing so, destroyed what was serious and important in the rite.

One of these is the cultural repudiation which has increasingly marked sections of the adult world itself since the eighteenth century—the reaction against the heritage of the past which characterises so many areas of scientific and artistic interest today. The *rite de passage* sought to induct into cultural modes and duties; it looked, of course, to the past as a standard. But science both pure and applied, perhaps naturally, as an essential element in the very structure of its proceedings, lives by

---

[1] *Essays in Ritual of Social Relations*, ed. M. Gluckman, pp. 56–57.

repudiating its own past; and so great is its prestige, that many of the arts, too, grasp after the new, the as yet unattained, and manifest an indignation against their own histories; how, otherwise, does one explain the proliferation of styles which mark so many fields of artistic endeavour, so that no sooner is one developed than it is rejected for the next extremity. (The Dada movement which underlies a great deal of what is produced in art today, was essentially an anti-art movement and created itself by repudiating the very art of former times on which it should have fed.)[1] Basically, the adult world here has lost its nerve, in the sense that it cannot feel deeply about what is passed on or consider sternly the means by which this can be done. It fears to be thought authoritarian—and it fears this more than it fears the helplessness of the young.

This fear is deeply affecting the rôle of the school as a place of initiation. Ideally, the school offers an induction into highly desirable adult rôles. It should stand as a bulwark against the enveloping tides of vulgarity from the community outside. It represents a range of valuable 'forms' into which the young can be initiated. Yet it, too, succumbs, in part, to the transvaluations of the world without. The whole progressive movement in education, for instance, is deeply imbued with Rousseau's and Dewey's anti-historicism; overtly, it places the emphasis on the child, and seeks an education which is restricted to his interests and momentary capacities to appreciate; or it brings into the foreground the temporary exigencies and eccentricities of current social policy. Furthermore, not only do important elements of the curriculum involve notions of flexibility, preparation for change rather than stability; but the very purpose of the school in our advanced industrial society is bound up with social mobility, with discontinuities of social experience. The aim of much current education involves the repudiation of the life-style of the father in order to gain an advantageous status for the children—who thus come to feel the superiority of their own standards to those of their parents. They are encouraged

[1] Cf. Hans Richter: *Dada*—an unconscious exposé of the childishness and banality of the movement.

Myth and the School Child

to challenge the continuity of social experience in the name of their own unavoidably shallow cultural experience. And highly educated adults, who should know better, accept too often this gesture of childish rebellion as their own.

No one would want to revive the barbarities of primitive initiation; but this loss of nerve of the adult community is a serious matter. It has allowed the infiltration of adolescent standards into the adult world—and what do such standards represent but the emotional instabilities, the inhibitions, the naïve acceptances and the repudiations of adolescence itself? It is little wonder that in such a situation one of the dominating myths has come to be that of romantic love, exploited by every advertiser and 'pop' singer, railway bookstall novelist and cheap newspaper; for it is precisely 'romantic' love that demonstrates those instabilities, those endless longings, that have replaced the coherence which it was formerly the function of myth and its attendent rituals to afford the life of the emotions and the social order it sustained.

For it *was* part of the function of the great myths of the past not only to create and reinforce social forms, to help in the crystallization of social attitudes, but to draw up lines of demarcation. Unsupported by the affective power of an explanatory mythology with its stern view of boundaries, the modern mind repudiates the notion of limitation; and we see this registered in the wider environment in the pervasive, but basically childish, view that the world provides an infinite reservoir of possibilities—both in impulse gratification and consumption.

For we should bear in mind, too, the sheer volume of vicarious experience by which our children are today encompassed. They can burn through a dozen dramas a week with ease, visit with all the power of visual presentation as many foreign lands, experience an incredible range of affective involvement. Even in the days of the cinema, Lawrence pointed out that a girl of eighteen thought she knew what it was to be in love, a deserted wife and a grandmother. It is little wonder that psychic as well as social mobility has become a characteristic of the modern world, the ability to project oneself into a wide variety of life-styles. The sheer volume of such involvement, indeed, may well induce a certain degree of emotional exhaustion as well as a false and unhealthy sophistication; so that the response to new, genuine experience is merely a cynical and indifferent 'We've been here before'.

Part of the result is that in the clarification of their existence, which is part of the function of any genuine education, young people today have to fight not only against natural ignorance but a quite wrong sort of knowledge.[1] The selectivity of art, which in a measure must be allowed to the meanest fictional representation in any medium, means that particular facets of vicarious experience can be conveyed with a peculiar intensity, which similar experiences are unlikely to achieve in life. The exploitation of so much of young people's fresh intensity by fictional material of such a low grade as the various media so often employ cannot but help make the whole business of growing up, which involves an induction into realities of great complexity, that much more difficult.

In its internal commitments, the school is devoted, in one of its guises, to the production of the 'thinking being', and with him to the scepticism which underlies his formation. Children are urged to think for themselves, in that peculiarly disintegrative form of thought which abstracts from a totality and fails to appreciate the limitations of taking the part for the whole. They are asked to make up their own minds, to question, to rely on their own judgments, above all not to accept. Such procedures have their negative as well as their positive side. What provides an analytical tool also induces a corroding scepticism; those who seek strong and healthy commitment in their pursuit of identity are afforded the hesitations of the analytical spirit. The 'free play of mind' is an admirable purpose, but it needs to

---

[1] Of course what is imbibed will vary from child to child in accordance with pre-disposition and previous experience and in accordance with what a child *brings* to the reading or viewing. cf. J. D. Halloran *The Effects of Mass Communication*. But all children bring some raw nerves to the situation (they used to be known as original sin), ready to be exacerbated by cheap, powerful, affective influences.

be exercised from a central core of assurance and acceptance. Even the socialization the school is now supposed to encourage springs out of abstractions about classlessness instead of the realities of a genuine social cohesiveness based on similarity of assumption and mind. In any school today a wide variety of historical traditions intermingle among its pupils; yet it can involve serious stress to offer too great violence to expectations which have been fostered in the very grain of family life and its supporting *lares* and *penates*.[1]

Where such strains of scepticism and individual responsibility are imposed on an, as yet, insecure self-image, is it to be wondered at that young people seek the affective comfort of the peer group and the 'pop' culture which supports it in a sort of effortless mindlessness? The school, too, needs to offer its participant rituals, its myths peculiar to its undertaking. Yet, even its minor ceremonies, like prize-givings, with their implicit celebration of achievement and attainment, are under attack, as are its assemblies for religious worship. That the latter are weak instruments in the face of the intellectual atomism the school is pledged to encourage, I would admit; but they can still leave behind their small legacies of participation in a purpose beyond the distribution of life chances, which is what the school's aim seems to have become. Plato thought we should manufacture myths, Hitler, for his evil purposes, showed that we could. Can nothing within the school replace the tawdry, evanescent myths of 'pop' in a way which would engage feeling as well as intellect? Or does the uncommitted quality of the school itself reflect a community where

> The best lack all conviction, while the worst
> Are full of passionate intensity!

At the very least, could not the school become fiercer, rather than more mild, in its qualitative demands? Must it try quite

[1] Some of the complexities involved in bringing together children from different classes and therefore from different sub-cultures with very different codes of behaviour in inter-sex relationships has been revealed in a recent article in *New Education* (May 1966) by D. Miller: 'Adolescence and Comprehensives'.

so hard to dissolve its image into the surrounding mush of egalitarian formlessness? Could it not celebrate its commitment to an older ethic, implying restraint for a long-term gain, a little more convincingly? For, if Professor McLuhan is right to urge, in metaphors drawn from our times, that 'sheer data processing confronts the ordinary child with a situation of information overload' in this electronic era, the school must be prepared to offer him, with some affective force, concepts and categories, forms and models in terms of which he can interpret and assess some, at least, of the multifarious media presentations.[1] And this must, with many, become central, not peripheral.[2]

[1] There is no need, yet, as I see it, to succumb to Professor McLuhan's pessimistic assessment: 'The psychic strategies needed to cope with information overload make the curriculum and the classroom seem ludicrous and 'square' to young people accustomed to T.V. and the electronic environment'. And, indeed, his surrender to the concept of 'all-at-onceness' as the characteristic cultural form of our times involves the implication that 'experience' has been reduced to senseless flux. Though the categories are admittedly more fluid than they once were, they still have currency as interpretative models, if only the adult world can keep (or recover) its *élan*. For what is at stake is the substitution of one model for another, not a complete formlessness: and the values implicit in different models of conduct and behaviour are at least *arguable*; though we should perhaps depend more on good *habits*, with their implications of authoritative handling in the early years, than we do.

[2] On the importance and pervasive presence of 'ceremonies' in school life cf. Willard Waller: *The Sociology of Teaching*, chapters 9 and 10.

5

The Implications of Literacy[1]

I have chosen to speak tonight of literacy, for literacy is the foundation of our system of education. Some words of D. H. Lawrence on this subject have haunted me for a long time. They appear in the *Fantasia of the Unconscious: The great mass of humanity should never learn to read and write—never.* Lawrence thought well of this sentence, for he put it in italics. Why he spoke in this way comes out in the body of his work. It has to do with the development of self-consciousness and the rôle of abstract thinking in our culture. He wished to assert different, and, to him, more satisfying modes of consciousness—sensuous modes which the proliferation of print has tended to inhibit.

I am not, however, specifically interested in Lawrence. Furthermore, let me allay, immediately, any suspicions that this lecture is going to degenerate into a nostalgic salute to a preliterate 'organic' community. My sole reason for quoting Lawrence lies in the jolt to the attention he provides. If one of the most penetrating critics of the modern world finds in a print culture evidence of psychic dislocation among that section of the population he knew best by right of birth—the working classes, the last to learn to read and write—how do we justify our stress on universal literacy? For, indeed, Lawrence does draw attention, dramatically, to a very odd feature of our educational system. It is intended to impose literacy on a total population —a thing which, so far as I know, no other civilization has tried to do. It is barely ninety years since education finally

[1] An Inaugural lecture delivered in the University of Leicester 19 October 1965. (Slightly shortened.)

became compulsory in this country; and a system of schooling intended to lead to universal literacy is becoming rapidly implemented in many other countries of Africa and Asia today. It is astonishing how little curious we are about this highly idiosyncratic feature of our education, how little interested we are in its psychic consequences. So I want to begin by asking what it *means* to learn to read and write—especially, to read. What modifications of consciousness are implied in the constantly exercised ability to interpret markings of the phonetic alphabet imprinted on papers bound together in easily portable form, which constitutes the ability to read as our society understands the skill? It is not the capacity painfully to spell out occasional manifestations of reading matter that I am concerned about, but reading as an assured and constant element in modern man's equipment, the aim, indeed, behind the educational demand. What is also understood by this demand, of course, is that what is read shall be of some quality.

Before I answer my own question, I must make it clear that my interest in print as a medium is related to two other fields of speculation which anyone involved in education is likely to become concerned about. There is, first, the problem of identity. How, and by what means, do people come to achieve a sense of personal identity in our advanced industrial society? Identity, after all, implies fixed characteristics, and our society is marked by social and psychological mobility and intellectual fluidity. Tentativeness replaces the authoritative; flexibility and the unfettered mind supersede the fixed point of view; the impermanent 'model' provides the paradigm of conceptual thinking. The range of social and vicarious experience open to us has immensely increased; democratic instability and media exposure have contributed to a certain psychic rootlessness. I have become particularly interested in trying to assess what part the various cultural media play in making us what we become. And, of course, print has developed into the first, historically speaking, of the mass media.

My second concern is the rôle and function of 'myth'. Much of what the various media convey is affective in nature; and,

The Implications of Literacy

indeed, by 'myth' I refer to ways of explaining certain non-rational areas of human experience, ways which traditionally have sustained important aspects of man's identity. In the past 'myth' has aided human orientation in a puzzling universe. It has had, too, implications for behaviour and conduct. In origins it is essentially a feature of communal life, but in our liberal society myth has tended to become fragmented—more a matter of private discovery and individual acceptance of explanatory models in these non-rational areas. Yet some communal mythological thinking does persist, secularized, of course, and can be put to dubious uses, as the modern dictator[1] and the advertiser, in their different ways, prove. In the diffusion of contemporary myth, print has had an important part to play—though in our century other media seem to make a wider impact.

My main concern, at first, however, is the rôle of print; and so I want to begin by considering the characteristics of the book purely as a medium—apart, that is, from any specific contents any individual book might contain. What modifications of man's experience, then, did Johann Gutenberg's revolution of the mid-fifteenth century—the invention of movable type—introduce into what had been primarily a preliterate, aural world, when dependence on manuscripts restricted the audience for books to the comparatively few? For it must be remembered that the appearance of new media of communication through technical advance introduces subtle modifications into social relationships and the individual consciousness of men. As Professor Marshall McLuhan has pointed out, the effects of technology do not only occur 'at the level of opinions or concepts, but alter sense ratios or patterns of perception.'[2] In part, at least, we must accept his dictum that the 'medium is the message'; the precise nature of the medium exercises a strong degree of control over *exactly* what can be said by means of it.

A preliterate world is essentially one of small communities; when communication to an audience takes place, whether that

---

[1] Cf. Ernst Cassirer, *The Myth of the State* (New Haven, 1961), Ch. xviii.
[2] Cf. Marshall McLuhan, *Understanding Media* (London, 1964), p. 18.

of a ballad singer or teller of tales, the performer depends on face-to-face relationships. His activities are communal and dramatic, nonrepeatable in the sense in which any dramatic representation will depend, in some degree, on a unique reciprocity of performer and audience. At the same time, traditional expectations and the sharing in a largely unconscious manner of common assumptions and modes of feeling will not produce anything comparable to the 'originality' of the modern entertainment artist.[1] The 'performance'—which is, indeed, no performance in the modern sense, but largely (though not entirely) an utterance of the expected and the time-honoured— will be often impersonal, more a revelation of communal feeling transmitted through commonly accepted symbols, not consciously 'personalized' by the individual characteristics of the performer.[2] Furthermore, the aural world, as Mrs. Willa Muir points out in her *Living with Ballads*, is concerned with 'energies, not concepts'. The spoken or sung word 'seems to penetrate more immediately, more directly, into the underworld of feeling than the word looked at on the printed page.' The resonances of the voice speak more directly to the emotions, conjure up a world altogether more alert to the senses than does the word which is read in silence. With the coming of a print culture, words lose some of their traditional magic qualities. As Dr. J. C. Carothers puts it, when contrasting the preliterate world of the African with that of the Western European, 'rural Africans live largely in a world of sound—a world loaded with direct personal significance for the hearer—whereas the Western European lives much more in a visual world which is on the whole indifferent to him.'[3]

[1] Cf. S. Hall and P. Whannel, *The Popular Arts* (London, 1964), Ch. II.

[2] 'Primitive song . . . is a communal activity. . . . It is therefore to some degree the voice of a common consciousness, of what a whole society or a representative part of it feels on certain occasions, and we have no reason to doubt that it really does this, or that all its participants share its moods and accept its assumptions' (C. M. Bowra, *Primitive Song* (London, 1962, p. 32).) Of course, Dr. Bowra is speaking here of primitive tribes; but much the same is characteristic of small, folk, preliterate communities dependent on face-to-face communication.

[3] Cf. J. C. Carothers, 'Culture, Psychiatry and the Written Word', in *Psychiatry*, November 1959. At the same time, an actual study of various African languages indicates differing patterns of sense awareness implicit in

And he points to the fact that 'sounds are in a sense dynamic things, or at least are always indicators of dynamic things—of movements, events, activities, for which man, when largely unprotected from the hazards of life in the bush or the veldt, must be ever on the alert.'

The coming of the printed book as a means of communication gradually changes all this. Of course, there is an important element of consciousness in the traditional oral epics, tales and ballads, for feeling is not simply expressed but articulated.[1] But there is no great concern, for instance, for originality of plot or story. Feeling is projected into a communally acceptable set of incidents and happenings which are expressions of general interests and awareness. The stories are usually well known: it is the rhetorical thrust or rhythmic ingenuity that holds the attention. At the simpler levels reinforcement and repetition rather than amplification and enlargement are the characteristic modes.[2] It is as if the feeling flows into what is already known, making the world more acceptable because its characteristic features are recognized and faced rather than that new areas of feeling are being constantly explored or revealed. For instance, it is only very slowly, over many centuries, that what Mrs. Muir terms self-consciousness entered the ballad form at all. Traditionally, their morality is that of the proverb and the traditional law, conventional, impersonal but often profound.

But the book is the instrument of self-consciousness. It points forward to personal, private satisfactions, the creation of individual mythologies in contrast to the oral, communal offerings. The social distance between creator and audience is immensely widened, for the book comes with none of the aural resonances

---

the languages themselves. One language, for instance, I am told, stresses taste much more than hearing; this would seem to advise caution in generalizing too glibly about the African's sense of reality.

[1] Thus Dr. Bowra points out that, communal in origin though so much of primitive song is, there is an important element of artistry in the work of the singer 'because he reduces his stirring thoughts to order and makes them as effective and attractive as he can' (*op. cit.*, p. 88).

[2] '. . . repetition, in one form or another, is common to primitive song. Indeed, it is more than common, it is fundamental': *ibid.*, p. 77.

of social life, but as a private possession, portable, repeatable, the inhabitant essentially of the study, the room set apart from family living. With the appearance of the book, reading becomes silent reading rather than the muttering which normally marked medieval attempts to read from manuscript. The book is a technical product, the result of indefinitely repeatable processes which cannot be shaped to the individual reader or group. The words come with none of the overtones and emphases of speech but rely totally on individual interpretation by the student. Sound, in fact, is translated into visual marks and interpreted by means of an internal dialogue: the reader is alone with such implication as he can inwardly construe. 'When words are written,' Dr. Carothers says,

> 'they become part of the visual world. Like most of the elements of . . . the visual world, they become static things and lose, as such, the dynamism which is so characteristic of the auditory world in general, and of the spoken word in particular . . . They lose . . . emotional overtones and emphases . . . Thus, in general, words, by becoming visible, join a world of relative indifference to the viewer—a world from which the magic 'power' of the word has been abstrated.'[1]

What seems to happen is that both the implications of the words and the incidents and happenings which the words serve to articulate become more individual to the writer and private. Language is used in increasingly idiosyncratic ways—the stock epithet of the preliterate communication disappears, for instance, and is replaced by a personally chosen word as new possibilities of experience are opened up; the great archetypal themes of a communal poetry become elaborated, personalized, projected into an individually chosen set of symbols. The social myths are replaced by a number of more individualized thematic treatments which increasingly are concerned with unique response to the archetypal situation.

The book and its contents, then, become individual possessions. We can see something of how the consequences of a developing print culture impressed an acute observer in

---

[1] Cf. Note 3 above, p. 114.

The Implications of Literacy

Shakespeare's *Hamlet*. The rapid growth of the reading public was a marked feature of Elizabethan England, as one of our most recent honorary graduates clearly demonstrated in his *Middle Class Culture in Elizabethan England*.[1] Shakespeare's insistence that Hamlet is a scholar of Wittenberg has implications other than that of involving the current Protestant-Catholic controversy about ghosts in his drama.[2] Hamlet is presented as a reader: 'But look where sadly the poor wretch comes reading,' the Queen says before leaving Polonius alone with her son:

> What do you read, my lord?
> Words, words, words.

In the very heat of his meeting with the ghost of his father, Hamlet's speech translates into an imagery appropriate to scholarship, print and authorship:

> Remember thee?
> Yea, from the table of my memory
> I'll wipe away all trivial fond records,
> All saws of books, all forms, all pressures past
> That youth and observation copied there,
> And thy commandment all alone shall live
> Within the book and volume of my brain
> Unmixed with baser matter—yes, by heaven! . . .
> My tables, meet it is I set it down
> That one may smile, and smile, and be a villain . . .

For, indeed, Hamlet displays precisely the inwardness Shakespeare must have recognized as characteristic of the reader and scholar. He does not make easy contact, except with his close friends and inferiors. Resolution, action, the immediate refuge of non-literate peoples, is in him 'sicklied o'er with the pale cast of thought': his hesitancy, his demand for proof ('that would be scann'd'), his reserve, even his Protestantism, all point to that interest in individuality which has come to be one of the defining characteristics of a book culture. Admittedly, there is

---

[1] Dr. Louis B. Wright.
[2] Wittenberg, Hamlet's university, in addition to its associations with Luther, had also a reputation for scholarship.

in Hamlet a quasi-pathological element which is no essential part of a book culture—but of that more anon.

Print, I have already suggested, relies on sight and the increasing dependence on visualization helps to foster social distance between people.[1] Hearing involves total immersion, for sound plays on all sides, but the visual exists only in a frame. Sight, indeed, implies the picture from which one is easily detached, as habituation to a print culture may have contributed to the evolution of the picture stage from the more nearly total involvement of the Shakespearean theatre, when the oral tradition was still very much alive. I was always puzzled as to why Hamlet needed to demonstrate the relative virtues of his uncle and father to his mother with 'pictures', until I realized that he is deeply involved with neither; it is at his mother, who is the real centre of his disturbance, that he wags his 'tongue in noise so rude'. 'Have you eyes?' he asks her, a question of profound psychic significance in view of his emotional state— unmistakably an Oedipus situation. The visual, here, implies detachment; he wants to deny her love for either.

It is not for nothing that *Hamlet* has been seen as marking a

---

[1] On this whole question of the changeover from the oral to the written and its effects on Western culture, the reader is referred to two extremely interesting articles by Father Walter J. Ong, S.J.: 'System, Space and Intellect in Renaissance Symbolism' in *Bibliothèque d'Humanisme et Renaissance*, Vol. XVIII (1956), pp. 222–239, and 'Ramist Method and the Commercial Mind' in *Studies in the Renaissance*, Vol. VIII (1961); also to his book, *Ramus: Method and the Decay of Dialogue* (Harvard, 1959). Father Ong's thesis is that 'In many ways, the greatest shift in the way of conceiving knowledge between the ancient and the modern world takes place in the movement from a pole where knowledge is conceived of in terms of discourse and hearing and persons to one where it is conceived of in terms of observation and sight and objects.' He treats the development of printing itself as a manifestation of a general reorientation of thought and attitude, especially in the field of logic, that was going on in the later medieval period: 'The use of printing need not be regarded as the cause of this shift in the focus of knowledge towards spatial analogies, but rather as a spectacular symptom of the general reorientation going on.' Nevertheless, the effect of printing was to give a great impetus to the process of increasing pictorialization and localization in space: 'Printing made the location of words on a page the same in every copy of a particular edition, giving a text a fixed home in space impossible even to imagine effectively in a pretypographical culture.' Marshall McLuhan's *The Gutenberg Galaxy* represents a further working out of Father Ong's thesis.

The Implications of Literacy

decisive stage in the development of Western self-consciousness. And, indeed, a proliferation of print produces the inner-directed detached being in ever greater numbers and the consequence is a growing social separateness. If the organic community ever existed, which I doubt, it does so no longer. What Professor McLuhan refers to as 'detribalization, individualization and pictorialization' are all facets of a similar process. Furthermore, the impact of the book was linear and successive rather than simultaneous. The spoken word must make a total impact, in response simultaneously to story, tone, emphasis, emotion. A Shakespeare play had to be grasped at a hearing; yet an aurally trained audience seems to have been capable of responding to recurrencies of imagery and juxtapositions which nineteenth-century criticism missed though based on a close reading of the text. The extent to which the book encourages the sequential and the linear can be judged when it is remembered that it also offered an infinite number of repeat performances. Repeatability, indeed, characterizes a book culture in two senses: an opportunity is offered the individual reader to look forwards and backwards, to ponder and repeat; and the same message can be shared by people remote in time and place. The book is both portable and transportable; it offers large opportunities of democratic extension. Hence thought becomes diffused to an extent impossible with a manuscript culture.[1] Hence, too, grammatical and orthographic standardization. Print, as H. J. Chaytor pointed out, follows after the development of the spoken language and imposes a literary turn of phrase often far removed from current modes of speech.[2] Correct spelling, in the popular mind, has come to symbolize the benefits of education, though because such correctness stems from the book it is often quite irrational in terms of the sound of the language. Yet, 'when speech and orthography fail to agree, script or print usually

[1] At the same time, one must not totally underestimate the capacity of even manuscript for a fair degree of diffusion. More copies of manuscripts were made than is sometimes suspected: Pliny the Younger, soon after 100 A.D., refers to a thousand copies of one manuscript being made. (W. Ivins, *Prints and Visual Communications*, p. 2.)

[2] Cf. *From Script to Print* (Cambridge, 1945).

gain the upper hand.' Such standardization is also an important factor in the development of a sense of national identity, as uniformity spreads throughout a particular linguistic area.

Furthermore, the development of a print culture has inevitably effects on writing. Logic and structure come to dominate over tone and feeling. The fact that the reader could go back and compare what was being said with what had gone before helped in the clarification of sense to the exclusion of other possible resonances. Punctuation comes to help sense, it is no longer an aid to breathing;[1] rhetoric tends to be replaced by a 'mathematical plainness'—there are other influences at stake, of course—words are valued for what they refer to rather than for their overtones and aural nuances. Writing, of course, demands also a much greater degree of inwardness than does speech. One needs to carry in the head awareness of before and after so that present writing will stand up to the close logical scrutiny that the repeatability of a print culture will allow. At the same time, except for those who have an exceptional ear, as gradually comes to be the prerogative of specialists called poets, structural qualities will be preferred to aural vividness: 'The mere act of inditing,' as Edgar Allan Poe put it, 'tends in a great degree to the logicalization of thought'.[2]

A certain narrowing of experience, then, is one of the consequences of a print culture. By 'narrowing' of experience I mean that we stress only certain aspects out of the totality which our senses present to us. The translation of oral symbols into visual abstractions—which is print culture—helps to exclude from sense a whole range of meanings which can only with difficulty be rediscovered in the inner ear; hence our general insensitivity to verse, and the difficulty we have in making poetry in a tone-deaf world. It was perhaps part of Shakespeare's good luck that he lived in an ambiguous age, when the oral tradition was still much alive and yet he was able to draw on the enlargement of

---

[1] Cf. W. J. Ong, 'Historical Background of Elizabethan and Jacobean Punctuation Theory' in *Publications of the Modern Language Association of America*, Vol. LIX (1944).

[2] Quoted in M. McLuhan, *The Gutenberg Galaxy* (London, 1962).

The Implications of Literacy

experience in that other sense which a print culture increasingly implied.

For, of course, though a print culture tended to narrow experience to one level by limiting the area of sense involved in a reading, the inwardness it stimulated extended experience in other ways. What has been lost in sensuous range (except by the few who have developed poetry as a highly specialized concern) has been made up in the amplification of possible psychic identity. I have already referred to the way in which communal mythology has gradually come to be replaced by individual, though fragmentary, explorations of areas previously inhabited by the simple tribal archetypes. The rapid circulation of books— repeatability in this sense—has meant the multiplication of vicarious possibilities. A print culture offers a multiplicity of identities; it tremendously increases the range of possible empathy. The rapid growth in the number of books was an essential preamble to that personal psychic mobility and acceptance of change which have almost come to be the defining characteristics of modern man.[1]

For what happens in this 'inward' fostered by print? If the book is the agent of individualism, of privacy (so that things come to happen 'in the mind'[2]), what happens within the new

---

[1] As, indeed, it is so treated in a fascinating study of what could almost be regarded as a process of detribalization on a vast scale, Daniel Lerner's *The Passing of Traditional Society: Modernizing the Middle East* (New York, 1964). The 'mobile sensibility' brought about by media exposure becomes Professor Lerner's criterion for entry into the modern 'participant' society. The traditionals are characterized by an inability to project themselves into other ways of life, to conceive of living ever in places other than their native villages; they are represented by the Turkish peasant who, when asked what he would do if he were made President, replied, in confusion, 'My God! How can you ask such a thing? How can I . . . I cannot . . . president of Turkey . . . master of the whole world?' If allowance is made for Professor Lerner's own rather naïve acceptance of the desirability of the whole process, the book provides a most interesting account of rapid modernization in psychological as well as technological terms—of awakened desires (cf. pp. 72–73) which are at once the hope and the snare of modern man.

[2] Knowledge comes to be thought of as being 'contained' in books and hence could be contained 'in the mind'. 'What you are thinking is now less than ever what you are holding converse with yourself about. It is simply what is "in your mind" ' (W. J. Ong, 'System, Space and Intellect in Renaissance Symbolism', p. 230).

The Implications of Literacy

dimension that has been added to personality? A wider gap, perhaps, between self and not-self, into which can flood a whole new range of possible selves—this, too, is part of the Hamlet experience. The famous speech: 'What a piece of work is a man' makes self-conscious the philosopher's awareness of man's multiplicity. In his heightened self-consciousness, Hamlet sees himself in a variety of rôles: the unplayable instrument, the 'rogue and peasant slave,' 'John-a-dreams'—and so on. As literacy has spread, the search for identity has become one of the obsessive themes of English literature. The comparative stability of personality implied in a traditional society, with its communally accepted mythological figures to act as social *paradeigmata* of acceptable behaviour, gives way to an increasing psychic rootlessness in face of the multiplying models for conduct that a book culture provides.[1]

I must add a few words here about the psychic function of myth, a term I have used on several occasions in this lecture.[2] The origin of myth lies in man's capacity to project many of his longings and desires, fears and dreads, aspects of his emotional life, into communally acceptable forms. Originally, 'myth' was always conceived of as dealing with realities, its function being to 'reveal the exemplary models for all human rites and all significant activities—diet or marriage, work or education, art or wisdom.'[3] Myths, in fact, became the communally shared ways of coping with many of more primitive man's inner tensions, hopes and fears; and they constitute the paradigms of many significant human acts, providing acceptable models for conduct. Men in archaic societies were obliged not simply to remember mythical history, but to re-enact it; it both externalizes significant areas of human experience and provides a pedagogic image: 'Life produces myth and finally imitates

[1] Cf. Lerner, *op. cit.*
[2] On the question of myth, the reader is referred to the works of Ernst Cassirer, *Philosophy of Symbolic Forms*, Vol. II: *Mythical Thought* (New Haven, 1955); *The Myth of the State; Language and Myth* (New York, 1946); and cf. also Susanne Langer, *Philosophy in a New Key* (Cambridge, Mass., 1960), Ch. VII; Mircea Eliade, *Myth and Reality* (London, 1963).
[3] Eliade, *op. cit.*, p. 8.

The Implications of Literacy

it'.[1] Man's attempt, in fact, was to live his myth. He both possessed and was possessed by it.

Originally, then, myth was an *organ* of reality; it did not allude to something which was thought to exist independently of itself, but was a means of apprehending the thing-in-itself: 'Where we see mere representation, myth . . . sees real identity. The 'image' does not represent the thing; it *is* the thing.'[2] With the development of civilization, of course, myth came under rationalist attack—among the Greeks, for instance, by the time of Thucidydes, '*mythodes*' had come to mean 'fabulous and unauthenticated'; myth becomes allegory. Nevertheless, the model for imitation, the *paradeigma*, derived from the heroic legends, remains a fundamental concept in Greek education. Even Plato, in one sense the great enemy of the mythical in favour of the ethical based on reason, appreciates the seriousness of the heroic legends and seeks to ban unprepossessing tales of the Gods from his ethical *Republic*. In the *Laws*, he freely admits the power of the irrational, seeing in songs 'spells for the soul,' and admitting for the bulk of the population the prepotence of the emotional.

Now, what has all this to do with the development of a print culture? Two things. In the first place, it is important to realize that with the coming of first a manuscript and then a print culture the power of myth has been diffused, but not destroyed; and, secondly, that this power has become manifest in a confusing array of possible identities presented through the vast multiplication of books, of vicarious experiences, which a print culture has witnessed. In relation to my first point, it is interesting to realize that it was through the agency of print that many of the great myths of antiquity re-entered and captured the European consciousness. As Mircea Eliade puts it:

'Through *culture*, a de-sacralized religious universe and a de-mythicized mythology formed and nourished Western

---

[1] Cf. Jerome S. Bruner, *On Knowing* (New York, 1965). I encountered Professor Bruner's book after I had completed the first draft of this lecture, and was interested to discover how some of his speculations paralleled my own.

[2] Ernst Cassirer, *Philosophy of Symbolic Forms*, Vol. II, p. 38.

civilization—that is, the only civilization that has succeeded in becoming exemplary . . . The victory is that of the *book* over oral tradition, of the document—especially of the written document—over a living experience, whose only means of expression were preliterary.'[1]

What happens psychically is both the codification of memory—history becomes an increasingly precise study, implying radically different customs and habits for study and introjection—and the amplification of social empathy. What is being prepared is an increasing psychic rootlessness. The gain is an immense extension of sympathy, the loss a certain confusion in the achievement of identity.

I have spoken earlier of books as possessions; but in certain cases they have retained the mythical power to possess; we have, indeed, just seen how, through the diffusion of print, the European consciousness became, for several centuries, possessed by classical models.[2] Exposure to books widens horizons, but has, in extreme cases, a pathological effect. The inwardness a book culture encourages becomes the scene of a private drama: the man can both possess and be possessed by the contents. There is, of course, nothing particularly esoteric about this notion; man must always, in large part, live in terms of the social experience he has inherited and that he finds around him. Books are merely an extension of this understanding, abstractions from and distillations of experience. The process is analogous to that which Professor Gombrich noticed as characteristic of artistic creation: 'making comes before matching,' by which Gombrich meant that painters lived even more in terms of the conventions of their art than they did in relation to the 'real' visible world they intended to depict.[3] We all tend to structure the world in

---

[1] Eliade, *op. cit.*, p. 157.

[2] Cf. W. J. Ong, 'System, Space and Intellect in Renaissance Symbolism'. 'When the humanists attempt a retreat into classical antiquity, their very reason for doing so and their way of conceiving their manoeuvre reveal them as men of the Gutenberg era. Erasmus' and others' assertion that all the knowledge possible to man is contained in the writings of the ancients clearly manifests the spatialized understanding of knowledge typical of medieval man' (p. 230).

[3] Cf. E. Gombrich, *Art and Illusion* (London, 1962), and *Meditations on a Hobby Horse* (London, 1963), Ch. 1.

The Implications of Literacy

terms of the concepts, models, conventions we have inherited. A myth, as we have seen, was, in general, a very early method of structuring areas of human awareness relevant to the sort of experience myth was intended to explain. If Christopher Caudwell is right to urge—and I believe in some degree he is—that 'the world of literary art is the world of tribal mythology become sophisticated and complex and self-conscious,'[1] then this does not mean that man is 'freed' from the incubus or support of myth (whichever way one likes to look at it), but that the attempt to carve out an identity, which myth aided at the level of the tribal structure, becomes matter for inward struggle and tension. Books, then, immensely complicate the process—they do not fundamentally change it. Nor is it only literary experience that complicates life. Social and political theories, for instance, have, as Georges Sorel has pointed out, also assumed mythical characteristics in our era; they, as well as the symbols, allegories or images of imaginative compositions, have helped to form—or confuse—man's identity-in-action.

Literary artists themselves have noted the extent to which reading-matter can, in extreme cases, provide the material for what is almost a form of neurotic possession. If the great prize of a book culture is the extension of consciousness it involves, a sort of detached empathy, a 'free play of mind,' not all devoted readers achieve such a consummation. In the earlier days of the Gutenberg era most of the output of the printing presses was devoted to copies of medieval books. One possible consequence can perhaps be seen in *Don Quixote*:

> 'In short, he so buried himself in his books that he spent the nights reading from twilight till daybreak and the days from dawn till dark; and so from little sleep and much reading, his brain dried up and he lost his wits. He filled his mind with all that he read in them, with enchantments, quarrels, battles, challenges, wounds, wooings, loves, torments and other impossible nonsense; and so deeply did he steep his imagination in the belief that all the fanciful stuff he read was true, that to his mind no history in the world was more authentic.'

[1] Christopher Caudwell, *Art and Reality*.

The Implications of Literacy

Stendhal, in *Le Rouge et le Noir*, creates someone who lives largely in terms of the quasi-mythical representation of an historical figure he has absorbed from his reading. Julien Sorel, indeed, provides an admirable example of someone whose many actions are dictated by the image of an identity he has acquired from study; even his love-making comes to be a duty he has imposed on himself so that he can live up to the Napoleonic yearnings he has derived from his reading. The explanation, of course, is fairly simple. Many obscure attitudes and latent feelings only come to light when they are articulated through a given rhetoric.[1] Any extension of consciousness involves the ambivalence implicit in the thoughts and feelings aroused: the publication of *Werther*, for instance, led to a wave of suicides.

Certainly, we must not forget those obscure Judes to whom the extension of consciousness implicit in a book culture added a new dimension to their beings—the lives of many such were narrow and frustrated for lack of the learning and reading for which they craved—yet 'we must remember,' as T. S. Eliot said, 'that being more conscious about everything is a very great strain'. And one of the great themes of modern literature is that of initiation into consciousness and the consequences for identity such initiation involves. It appears in Henry James, for instance, in the contrast of American simplicity and European cultural complexity; D. H. Lawrence deals with it in *The Rainbow*, when the Brangwens, through the pertinacity of the womenfolk, seek 'this education, this higher form of being that the mother wished to give to her children, so that they, too, could live the supreme life on earth.'

And yet, for all their realization of ambiguity and hesitation, the answer of writers of this stature is, in the final analysis, unequivocal: 'we are committed to more consciousness.' Of course, we have to accept the challenge of literacy. But we must do so with a much clearer view of what is involved than we have at the moment. That is why I have tried to indicate a few of the

[1] An interesting study of this phenomenon is to be found in Denis de Rougemont, *Passion and Society* (London, 1940), where the author traces the effects of the Tristan myth of romantic passion on the European consciousness. Cf. Chapter 4.

The Implications of Literacy

complexities implicit in this literacy into which we seek to induct all our children. The ultimate purpose of education—any education—I take to be clarification of the world of nature, of the world of man, and of the internal world of sensation and reflection, of emotion and cognition. Today, that clarification can be achieved by direct experience *and* through the accumulated experience of others conveyed through our book culture; we need the fullest possible interaction between the two and this implies a high degree of conscious awareness, of interplay between what is read and what is lived.

The maintenance of these antinomies is a problem large enough even in a propitious environment; but the environment is not propitious. At a time when we are attempting to raise the level of consciousness of a whole people through the agency of this particular culture—that of books and literacy—alternative cultural media, implying different sense ratios, complicate our task; at a time when what we should be seeking is clarification, commercialism and the image-making that commercialism involves threaten us. Let me explain more fully.

One consequence of our print culture is the development of a closely integrated technological society—for, of course, without the rapidity of intellectual communication that print permits, technical change on the scale we have seen it would have been impossible.[1] As part of that technical change we have seen the development of new mass media of communication—new electric media I shall call them—radio, cinema, television. Their social and psychological implications are different from those of a book culture. Individualistic liberalism is the fine flower of a book culture, with its dependence on withdrawal and privacy; the new media are more communal because their particular forms of mass, mechanical, simultaneous communication imply audience stereotypes which, in the end, they must create as a condition of acceptance. Psychologically, they encourage a dispersal of attention because they work on the assumption that

[1] The ability to reproduce pictures and sketches by means of print has played a vital part in our technical development, for instance, 'Without pictures, most of our modern highly developed technologies could not exist' (W. Ivins, *Prints and Visual Communications*, p. 100).

concentration is weak and fleeting and that, therefore, prolonged demands on it—typical of a book culture—are to be
avoided. (The modern popular newspaper—print reduced to a
mass medium—shows much the same tendency.) Where the
balance of the senses is concerned, there is a tendency to rein-
state the aural—with radio, especially, of course; their strongest
cultural characteristic is probably that of actuality, of contem-
poraneous participation. They tailor the present for mass consumption. Hence their collectivist implications. In general, they
don't imply any profound internal dialogue but an attention to
surface detail, an ability to capture the fortuitous or the acci-
dental, the transitory, the chance collocation. The essence of
cinema, for instance, is movement; its art is that which brings
apparently chance images into significant juxtaposition. It is
essentially an art of surface, two-dimensional.[1] Yet all the
electric media, of course, contain a certain qualitative potential
which is sometimes fulfilled.

My point, in this wildly superficial treatment of significantly
different media, is but to convey that there may well be some
degree of disharmony between the serious book culture of the
school—qualitative print culture—and the characteristic electric
media of the non-school environment. Psychologically, they pull
in different ways. Furthermore, the mass media in their typical
manifestations are, in varying degrees, bound up with commercialism and the economy. This has become true of print
also, now that it has developed, under the impact of commercial development, from a medium to a mass medium.[2]
Much of commercialism is anti-educative by nature. It is
often argued that we should educate for the expansion of

[1] Cf. Siegfried Kracauer, *Nature of Film* (London, 1961).
[2] The change is partly the result of the decay of patronage and the open-
ing up, since the eighteenth century, of a mass market. At the same time,
implicit in the development of the printing press was, of course, the com-
mercialization of literature: 'Dès l'origine l'imprimerie apparut comme une
industrie régie par les mêmes lois que les autres industries, et le livre une
marchandise que des hommes fabriquaient avant tout pour gagner leur vie'
(Febvre et Martin, *L'Apparition du livre*, p. 162). The development of the
reading public and its growing appetite for entertainment is traced in R. D.
Altick, *The English Common Reader* (Chicago, 1957).

the economy so that, in time, more people will be released for educational (meaning cultural) pursuits. What is not sufficiently appreciated is that commercialism and education as I have defined it in this lecture—as clarification, that is—are not compatible. Commercialism, for success, increasingly depends, not on the product offered for sale, but on the brand image. In its characteristic presentation to the public it seeks to stress, not the functional capabilities of the article but a set of psychologically relevant, but factually distorted, circumstances; the realism of photography, for instance, is exploited for lying purposes. Deep personal problems will not be solved by buying a bottle of X, and it is very doubtful if many days are actually *made* by Cadbury's Milk Tray. It is not enough to say that people know, cognitively, the distinction between the image and the reality; the appeal is primarily emotional, the aim to exploit the non-rational element in purchasing. Man's willingness to be deceived by appearances—a major theme of great literature—is the key to commercialism. It is little wonder that the schools are so ineffectual in their attempts at clarification.

Anyone who is appointed to profess Education should have some ideas concerning the nature of the activity he is appointed to profess and the obstacles and hindrances which are likely to get in the way of its more effective deployment. What I have said tonight is obviously in some measure speculative and I would readily admit to some failure of emphasis or some mistake of analysis. My aim has been to open up a theme, not to close it, to stimulate to further discussion, correction and amplification. What I will not readily concede, however, is that my theme is not central to our present system of education. Let me recapitulate briefly: imbued with certain views as to mankind's potential capacity for an extended rational awareness, the nineteenth century embarked on a policy of imposing a certain sort of culture, that based largely on print technology, on a total population; and this was, *par excellence*, the culture of the inner consciousness. My theme has been concerned with the psychological and social implications of this attempt at the spread of literacy; I think it will be admitted that, in a university, the very heart and centre of this culture of literacy, this is not an improper subject to open up.

It is more, indeed, than a proper question to ask—it is a pressing one. What has been apparent for a long time is that the education we provide produces on a considerable section of the population few or no results.[1] We are seeking to convey a culture—or, at the least, a somewhat watered-down version of it—a culture of a sort for which this section of the population is historically and psychologically ill-prepared, and which has few roots in the community from which its members spring. The proof of my contention lies in the nature of the popular culture into which the erstwhile scholars retreat once they leave school; and, in our inability to keep many of those even of tested good aptitude at school should they spring from unpropitious cultural circumstances.[2] To put it bluntly, many do not seem able to face up to the psychological demands of the kind of literate culture I have been talking about during this lecture. The pattern of their social life does not encourage the privacy and inwardness a book culture requires. They have lost their traditional oral way of living; the profounder demands of qualitative literacy make little appeal, induce, indeed, a widespread apathy, once the basic skills of reading and writing have been—often tardily—acquired. They become sitting targets

[1] America provides an even more startling proof of this contention. For quite a time, now, America has provided more years of schooling per head of the population than any other nation. Yet, if qualitative literacy has been the aim, it has proved a failure: 'Unlike his European counterparts, the American book-man has struck no roots in the national soil. This alienation is reflected in many ways: "A Gallup poll, published in February 1950, reports: 'Despite our mass education and high degree of literacy, the United States has the lowest proportion of book readers of any major democracy, judging by the results of an international survey in six nations . . . the United States brought up the rear, with only one adult in five reading a book.' " ' ('The Book Business in America,' Alan Deutscher, reprinted in *Mass Culture*, ed. Rosenberg and White (New York, 1964).)

[2] It is becoming apparent, for instance, that comprehensive schools are failing to convince some able working-class children that the culture of literacy has much to offer them. At any rate, they appear to have little more success in persuading certain children of good measured intelligence who come from working-class backgrounds to stay on at school than did the schools under the tripartite system.

The Implications of Literacy

for an affectively based, media-communicated culture, piped to them by people clever enough to exploit what 'education' has failed to give; and this at a time when work, for many, fails to provide any prolonged contact with the realities of materials and processes.

Indeed, I have spoken so far of the implications for identity of our book culture; but many of these culturally indifferent children are involved in the problem of multiplicity, too; *their* confusions arise from the offerings of the electric media or the cheapest writings, not the complex demands of qualitative literacy. It is worth noting, then, that today all sections of the community participate in the psychic mobility which is specifically characteristic of modernity. To that extent, the crisis of identity is universal. In this we are all equal. Educationally, we face a similar task with the whole school community at very different levels of attention and complexity.

And yet, the notion of equality, which is, at the moment, exercizing a powerful effect on educational policy, is being used to make more difficult any possibility of evolving a system of education adjusted to the varying levels of cultural and mental capacity in our community. That all should be afforded an equal opportunity to come to such fullness of themselves, to achieve such identity, as an organized system of education can afford, is a principle I completely accept. But, that all should be subjected to an identical diet in order to produce an unobtainable cultural homogeneity, invites educational disaster. As Dr. Bernstein implies, many children lack the sheer linguistic understanding to cope with the complex demands of the culture of literacy. His distinction between *public* and *formal* language systems is highly relevant to the thesis of this lecture.[1]

---

[1] The distinction is that between 'public,' the language of the lower working class, and 'formal,' that of the middle classes. In his essay on 'Social Class and Linguistic Development: A Theory of Social Learning' (republished in *Education, Economy and Society*, ed. Halsey, Floud and Anderson (New York, 1961)) Dr. Bernstein draws attention to the extent to which, in middle-class habits of upbringing, the process of individuation is accompanied by increasing verbal refinement. Thus is acquired a potential for a qualitative literary culture. The 'public' language of the working-class child (of which Dr. Bernstein gives an extended analysis) has none of these

The Implications of Literacy

Our debate on secondary and higher education, especially, it seems to me, needs to be carried on in terms of the fundamental cultural experience we are giving our young people. It is not being carried on in these terms; it is carried on in terms which are often more relevant to social and political considerations than they are to strictly educational ones. I will grant that in a state system of education social and political considerations cannot be wholly ignored; but they should loom less largely than they do.

It is, for instance, because of these implications of literacy I have explored tonight that I find myself highly critical of the move towards comprehensive secondary education, with its widespread provision of a common core curriculum in the earlier years. To me, the spread of comprehensive schooling is, at best, an irrelevance, in face of the profound problems that the imposition of universal literacy has faced us with. A limited number of children, by native ability combined with a favourable home environment of affection and concern, are suited to the exacting psychic demands that are made by a qualitative print culture; the others, through lack of innate aptitude uncompensated for by propitious home or environmental circumstances, afford a quite different cultural potential. They still need to acquire the basic tools of literacy which our closely knit, highly urbanized technological society requires. Once this has been done, a great deal of the ordinary culture of literacy, such as our schools are accustomed to provide, ought to be swept aside and discrimination relevant to the new electric media needs to be taught. Paradoxically, their ability to benefit from such tools of literacy as they have acquired will be improved by developing their consciousness through the characteristic cultural forms they daily encounter; if they come to appreciate better TV, better films, better radio, to participate in activities which involve them in the realities of materials and feelings (I have in

---

refinements. It is hardly surprising that the culture of literacy makes so little appeal to him. We have been unbelievably naïve to think the response could have been other than it actually has. Cf. also J. B. Mays, *Education and the Urban Child* (Liverpool, 1962).

mind work in various crafts, modern educational dance, drama, among others) they will increase their potential for enjoying and appreciating the books they will still, of course, be encouraged to read. The aim should be to raise a whole cultural level, as an interactive process, not to confine either to print or to the electric media. Furthermore, we must always keep open a door for later development.[1] But to try to inculcate a qualitative print culture without taking cognizance of the profoundly anti-educative forces implicit in so much of the mass media is to invite disaster. (I am not, of course, ignorant of the fact that, sporadically, some features of these suggestions exist in some schools already; I am aware of a new concern for the curriculum fostered by the Schools Council. But the time has come when we need to evolve a *systematic* theory of popular education. We need to become more aware of the possibility that in some respects our popular culture may well turn out to be a post-literate one.)

This is no attempt to put back the clock, to revert to Victorian notions of educating the worker in order to produce docile employees. But it is no service to any child, of whatever class, to pretend, for social and political purposes—even for humanitarian ones—that he is otherwise than he is. Indeed, questions of class are by no means always relevant. The determination of precisely what he is is a matter of great delicacy and subtlety; but, even with our present imperfect instruments of assessment, this can be more nearly determined than some people care to admit. Our aim must be to contribute (as far as schooling can) to a genuine life experience, not to offer the 'scraps, orts and greasy relics' of an unpalatable culture, however fine, in essence, that culture may be. We must offer all people an opportunity to realize themselves and in doing so we must submit to the immense variety of human talent by which we are challenged; changing social circumstances—better material conditions,

[1] We mustn't, either, fall into the opposing error of underrating the potential of some Secondary Modern children; cf. J. Adcock, *The Study of Narrative Prose in the Secondary Modern School* (Unpublished M.Ed. thesis, the University of Leicester). Mr. Adcock shows that some children can achieve more in the reading of good literature than is commonly assumed.

housing, food—may ameliorate but not abolish great dis-
crepancies of talent.

The well-meant sentimentality of the egalitarians inhibits
any such solution; I know it is well-meant because I have come
to respect the sincerity of many of them; but I speak of sentimentality, because their policies spring, not out of a genuine—
indeed, reverent—attempt to assess the potential of particular
children in relation to a specific socio-cultural environment, but
from highly abstract—one might even say, bookish—schemes
of human improvement which fail to accept the complexity of
human existence as it actually faces us. Our modern emphasis
on the principle of equality, indeed, illustrates the pathologies to
which a book culture is prone. Derived from the theorizing of
the Enlightenment, it had its relevance amidst the social
rigidities of the nineteenth and early twentieth centuries.
Today, it has sufficiently penetrated our consciousness to make
its further propagation unnecessary, not to say harmful, in the
changed situation that the notion of equality has itself brought
about. The abstract speculations of eighteenth-century *philoso-
phes* have little relevance to the profoundly different socio-
cultural conditions of our comparatively affluent industrial
society, with yet its profound crisis of identity and its addiction
to the qualitatively inferior and the lying image.

I am usually accused of conservatism; *my* 'image' is that of the
'backwoodsman'. I am pictured, no doubt in postures of patri-
cian ease, acquiring outmoded social attitudes along with
unspecified quantities of Madeira and nuts. It says so in the
Times Literary Supplement. I quote: '. . . his crusty attitude picked
up over the Madeira and nuts of the Leicester Education
Department one supposes . . .'[1] And this imputation of unbend-
ing rigidity is strange, because the implications of what I have
said tonight are, after all, revolutionary. I have suggested that
our thinking about education should be controlled by a profound awareness of the cultural demands we make on children
in relation to the curriculum we teach, for it is our culture which
serves to structure our intellectual and emotional life. I have

---

[1] *Times Literary Supplement*, 27 May 1965.

The Implications of Literacy

urged that a realistic appraisal of what we achieve in schools would suggest that much of our education is a failure. I have urged that clarification, including as one of its objectives a more adequate realization of personal identity, is the real task that faces us in education at all levels. Once thought of in these terms, and recognizing the multiplying agencies of image confusion that our commercial society has spawned, I have urged a fundamental reorientation of the whole curriculum for considerable sections of our school population. I have suggested that the widespread attention to secondary school reorganization which is at present laying waste the energies of the teaching population is an irrelevance. I have always deprecated change for the sake of change, the futile restlessness, the recurrent itch, the failure to measure up to the real educational issues. But perhaps I can claim that the views I have expressed here don't altogether suggest ossification.

6

The Rôle of the Teacher

I

Progressive, 'child-centred' theories of education offer the sharpest challenge to the traditional conception of the rôle of the teacher; and I will relate my exploration of how I conceive the teacher's function to views developed by the 'new' educators.

In considering the rôle of the teacher the sorts of metaphors and analogies which educationists use are often profoundly significant. Thus, Froebel, like so many of the earlier child-centred educationists, relies heavily on the 'plant' metaphor, the supposed analogy between the growth of trees and flowers and the development of a child. The implication is, that it is only necessary to give a child air and space, an environment, that is, within which he can expand, and he will inevitably grow in freedom; thus the job of the teacher is, as Froebel put it, to be 'passive and protective, not directive and interfering'. And, even today, when the need for social training is more fully realized, the intervention of the teacher in child-centred schools all too often stops once the more overt forms of social harmony have been induced. Herbart, on the other hand, used metaphors drawn from building, implying the arrangement, as it were, of brick on brick. He desired a very active rôle for the teacher, though he did not forget the need for activity on the part of the child. But it was the job of the teacher to present new knowledge, stimulate new interests, introduce experiences the child had not yet had, instead of merely following up those he already had undergone.

The Rôle of the Teacher

The fallacy of the Rousseau-Froebel line of thinking can, to my mind, be shown from the fact that these educationists were not consistent in the setting forth of their precepts. 'The great thing,' said Rousseau about the training of the under twelves, 'is to do nothing'. All the time, however, he is urging the need so to arrange the environment and the experiences the child is likely to encounter that only certain things shall strike the attention of Emile. And the rigidity of Froebel's gifts and occupations —apparatus intended to promote the creative and sensory development of children—is in strange contrast to his emphasis on pedagogical passivity. And I believe that the dilemma in which Froebel and Rousseau found themselves is one which must affect the child-centred educationist everywhere. For, after all, even in the most child-centred schools, activities are provided; the mere fact of having to attend school at all restricts freedom of choice, and once thirty or forty youngsters are congregated in a room, the range of activities they can undertake is essentially limited. Teachers in such schools, then, I find, often feel in a quandary. The theory bids them interfere as little as possible; all must come from the children. But, in effect, the activities are limited and are, in fact, most carefully chosen for their educative possibilities. What then are the limits on the teacher's intervention? Should this child be helped with his painting? Shall that one be permitted to undertake the same activity week after week, simply because that is what he wants to do? The situation is perplexing—and largely, I think, because it has been insufficiently thought out and clarified.

The fact of the matter is that the world of human beings displays at least one profound difference from Froebel's world of trees and plants; human beings are capable of gradually assuming a power of self-direction based on reason which is quite foreign to the natural world. This power of *self*-direction, is, however, paradoxically something which has to be acquired, as a result of insight based on training; it is not something we are born with. I think D. H. Lawrence had the crux of the matter when he said that he wanted 'living spontaneous individuality in every man and woman. This living spontaneous individuality, being the hardest thing of all to come at, will need most careful rearing.'

Thus it is right that, in teaching him, the child's powers and potentialities should be considered; this is the great benefit that child-centred education has bestowed on us. But the child himself does not, and cannot, fully realize what these potentialities are, because he can have no insight into the sorts of opportunities which the civilized life affords for their employment; and so that employment is not one the child can spontaneously come to. Careful nurturing, then, is necessary. Not only is it necessary to extend the range of the child's experience by presenting to him experiences which he is unlikely to encounter spontaneously but which are known to be valuable; it is also necessary to assist him to overcome the rebellious side of his nature which, as an observable fact, so often tends to jib at the self-denying discipline needed to master any complex human skill or knowledge. Let us use interest where possible, by all means; but it is unreasonable to assume that interesting stimulants can or should always be found to carry one over the drudgery which enters into all human acquirements. Many children, for instance, could benefit from learning to play a musical instrument. Is it reasonable to expect most children spontaneously to undertake the practice necessary for achievement? The benefits are remote; the scales and arpeggios are an all too immediate reality.

Furthermore, it is often necessary to protect the child, in our admass society, from influences which are likely to be cheapening and harmful. Child-centred theories tend to rest on the assumption of the natural goodness of man;[1] the child should develop uncontaminated if only left to express himself rather than the equivocal values of his times. But, of course, no such isolation is possible; the child is subject to social pressure from birth. So, whether we think the child is conceived in sin, or comes trailing clouds of glory, the evil is still there to be com-

[1] Though most progressives today, I think, if challenged, would urge the moral neutrality of the new-born. But the idea of natural goodness is in the tradition of progressivism.

The Rôle of the Teacher

batted. It is part of the function of the school to bring to bear the more desirable and exclude the less desirable features of our heritage in order to serve the ultimate good of the child. Now our thinking about education has, in recent years, been much bedevilled by the use of a vague, imprecise vocabulary. Thus, we have tended to think that if we only provide the right conditions for fostering 'growth', or 'development', the precise definition of what sort of growth or of development towards what, can be left conveniently vague, or blanketed under some such formula as 'wholeness' or 'well-balanced personality'. A great deal of attention, in the development of child psychology, has been directed to the facts of the educational situation—how children learn, what incentives are necessary, involving questions of technique—but far too little to the values which this proliferation of techniques is concerned to serve. Our society in general lacks a widely accepted view of what can be allowed to constitute an educated person and the partial abdication of the teacher's function which child-centred education involves springs, to some extent, from an insufficiently positive faith that some things matter and that our children should have an opportunity to acquire them. How often, for instance, in child-centred infant schools, have I noticed children cutting out crude pictures from the cheaper type of glossy magazine in pursuit of some project which, I have been assured, has been spontaneously asked for by the class. And yet there is some reason to believe that, even thus early, children's sense of line and colour is being destroyed by these influences.

For, indeed, the reason for my criticism of child-centred 'teaching' lies in the belief that 'learning', whether it is the acquiring of knowledge, skills or taste, matters. A supine acquiescence in the notion that happiness is the ultimate value has led us to underestimate the importance of achievement, even at a temporary loss of personal content. Child-centred education has been much imbued with the desire for happiness. The pursuit of truth, at whatever cost to oneself, and the consequent sense of sacrifice of self to something which exists independent of self, knowledge, is not encouraged by a theory

139

which assumes that the individual's impulses and desires form the sole criteria for educational concern. Hence the anti-academic bias one often notes among progressive educationists. Learning, of course, can degenerate into pedantry; but, at their best, the ordinary human fields of study offer an objective discipline which must be encountered on its own terms, and yet which affords the finest type of subjective enrichment. To remain centred on the self is, paradoxically, self-defeating; it is only the surrender to what is of value outside the self that is, in the end, satisfying. Children cannot possibly know this, but their teachers can. That is why the teacher, as a mediating functionary between the child and the world of learning, should play a positive, not a passive, rôle in the upbringing of the young.

II

What, however, is implied by a 'positive' rôle? Obviously this will, to large extent, be controlled by the nature of the subject-matter for which the teacher is agent, in terms of which he constitutes an 'authority'. But, often, the repudiation of the teacher's active participation in the pupil's learning situation springs, not so much from a realization of the need to recognize the differing demands made by different subject material, but from a reliance on the notion that it is morally objectionable for any personality to claim superior powers, even when it belongs to a teacher face to face with a class of young people. We can see this notion at work in a little book published some years ago by Professor R. S. Peters and called *Authority, Responsibility and Education*. In effect, Professor Peters' book contains an extended examination of the concept of 'having an education'. Sometimes this is implicit, sometimes it is explicit. Now, any conception of 'having an education' must include the notion of mental changes brought about through the conscious procedures adopted in some measure by another person; and because those procedures are conscious and the result of intent, the notion of morality is inseparable in any assessment of the changes so

The Rôle of the Teacher

wrought. A view of the good and a notion of effectiveness in action are part and parcel of the educator's conception of his job; and we find both elements in Professor Peters' exposition.

Let me begin, then, by making clear the particular moral viewpoint which informs Professor Peters' recommendations. It is that which one normally associates with present-day empiricist philosophers; it is, that is to say, Protestant, liberal, individualistic and, indeed, atomic. The moral agent it pictures is self-responsible, able to come to decisions on rational grounds, undetermined by previous personal—particularly childish—experiences or by any discoverable laws of historical necessity: the general effect of Freud and Marx, Professor Peters argues, is to make man more rather than less responsible. Knowledge of the circumstances increases rather than decreases our capacity to come to right moral decisions; for, indeed, the moral decision is to be made on this basis of the 'facts'; it is to be arrived at rationally, that is to say. And in arriving at a moral decision rationally, Professor Peters urges that circumstances of some sorts but certainly not *personalities* are relevant considerations. Actions cannot be condoned as the behaviour of particular individuals to whom special privilege belongs; moral decisions are based on equality of persons where, indeed, the context may be relevant but abstracted from any mystique of personality. Any charismatic aspect is to be looked upon as quite irrelevant in the making of moral judgments.

In putting forward this view of the nature of the moral decision, it is obvious that Professor Peters has been much influenced by a consideration of the procedures relevant in scientific learning and discovery. Indeed, he explicitly links together science and morality:

> Both science and morality (he urges) involve being reasonable or the use of reason . . . (This) means the determination to follow reasons and to disregard irrelevant considerations, or acting in accordance with certain procedures which are essential to discovering the truth . . . Just because *I* say this or *you* say that, it need not be right. The use of reason demands that differences or distinctions should only be made when there are *grounds* for making them.

This, for Professor Peters, provides the paradigm of the learning process. He constantly stresses the fact that it is the *manner* as much as the *matter* that is important in learning; and the manner to be adopted is one analogous to those employed in scientific learning and in arriving at moral decisions which I have just described . . . where, for instance, situations rather than personalities are the controlling factors.

Now, of course, what one wants primarily of a method of learning is that it shall be effective. However desirable the manner of procedure in some respects, if it does not promote learning it fails. And here, I think, Professor Peters trips up. For what, in effect, he is doing, I think, is to abstract a procedure which may well promote efficient learning in science, because such procedure is well adapted to the nature of the subject-matter in hand, and to recommend its adoption, no longer mainly on the grounds of efficiency, but primarily on those of morality, as a paradigm of the learning process. To put it another way, he confuses morality and effectiveness and he stresses the manner which is adapted to his view of morality, not that which promotes effective learning through careful adaptation to the subject in hand. And the basis of his morality lies in his repudiation, in social and political spheres as well as in educational, of the charismatic personality.

Now, I think that Professor Peters is mistaken in recommending on moral grounds procedures which should be considered mainly on the grounds of effectiveness: though I will grant that effectiveness and morality cannot be completely divorced, for, like all actions involving inter-human relationships, teaching methods need to be in line with acceptable moral principles. It is, perhaps, because I consider his view of the circumstances relevant to the making of moral decisions unduly narrow that I am willing to consider a much greater range of possible approaches to the learning situation. My view involves a different attitude to personality than that which he adopts; for it goes beyond what Miss Iris Murdoch has called that 'stripped and behaviouristic account of morality which the modern philosopher gives'. I shall take an example where the decision is

arrived at more on the basis of a morality which is, as Miss
Murdoch calls it, 'attached to the substance of the world', and
where an essential part of this substance is a view of human personalities and their interaction very different from that implicit
in Dr. Peters' account. In Emily Brontë's *Wuthering Heights*, the
elder Cathy marries Edgar Linton but remains attached by the
deepest springs of her being to Heathcliff. She explains her
inability to abide by the conventions of her marriage and des-
cribes Heathcliff in these terms:

> '. . . surely you and everybody have a notion that there is or
> should be an existence of yours beyond you. What were the use
> of my creation, if I were entirely contained here? My great
> miseries in this world have been Heathcliff's miseries, and I
> watched and felt each from the beginning: my great thought in
> living is himself. If all else perished, and *he* remained, *I* should
> still continue to be; and if all else remained, and he were annihi-
> lated, the universe would turn to a mighty stranger; like the
> foliage in the woods, time will change it, I'm well aware, as
> winter changes the trees. My love for Heathcliff resembles the
> eternal rocks beneath: a source of little visible delight, but
> necessary . . .'

In rational terms, she belongs to Edgar Linton; this is Nelly
Dean's opinion and Nelly Dean represents the common-sense
world. But Cathy's assertion of her attachment to Heathcliff
transcends the '*duty* and *humanity*', 'the *pity* and *charity*' that
characterizes, in Heathcliff's contemptuous terms, Edgar
Linton's more sober relationship with her. One of the points of
the book is that the Heathcliff-Cathy relationship challenges
the whole rationalistic liberal ethos of the nineteenth century
because it suggests an order of 'reality' where such purely
rational considerations are irrelevant. This is a morality associated with a metaphysic of man's nature removed from the
basis of reason and argument assumed by the modern empirical
philosopher—a philosopher like Dr. Peters who, symptomati-
cally, refers to the family in terms of an 'irrational bond of love
and loyalty'.

All this may seem remote from Professor Peters' tidy little
book on Authority in Education. I don't believe it is and I want

The Rôle of the Teacher

to go on to consider why. For one thing, the whole experience of *Wuthering Heights* seems to me to indicate forces at work in the effect of one personality on another which the rationalist either ignores or shudders away from. I said a few moments ago that Dr. Peters' paradigm of knowledge is science; and science, he asserts correctly, is anti-authoritarian in the sense that its appeal is always to facts and not to personalities. The moral enterprise of science is indeed at the opposite pole to that of love in human relationships—the arguments and evidence are every-thing and the human factor nothing or very little. Furthermore manner—method—in science is of fundamental importance; in love it is of little importance except to the professional sedu-cer. When Professor Peters wishes to support his emphasis on manner, he usually employs, as illustrations, examples drawn from learning which is dispositional: he talks of keeping chickens, carpentry, of 'thinking' rather than of an attachment to the objects of thought. In such learning the teacher becomes simply an intermediator; he points to the important elements in the situation and then allows the situation to do its work. Here, then, the progressive's distrust of personality may have a limited point; we can agree, that is, with Professor Peters when he urges that 'the task rather than the man exerts the discipline'. This, of course, looks back beyond Dewey to Rousseau, whose neurotic disgust with social life—with per-sonalities—led him to consider 'things' as more truly educative than 'men', and in doing so found allies in those seventeenth and eighteenth century educators who preferred 'things' to 'words'.

But, of course, not all learning is of this sort. For Professor Peters' is the learning appropriate to a practically-minded, sceptical age whose boasted toleration is often the off-shoot of lack of conviction rather than of any deep appreciation of the human predicament, whence it might derive at once the guts and conviction to hate the sin while maintaining a balance of generous sympathy ready to respond to the humanity of the sinner. Professor Peters' view of the educated man comes, today, to wear something of an old-fashioned look; though he

The Rôle of the Teacher

is in most respects so much superior to what may well replace him—the Organization Man—that one welcomes, to that extent, his resuscitation. Yet he was never an adequate figure for many in a mass society; and that he is being replaced results partly from the too restricted view of the dimensions of human personality out of which he was formed, particularly of what, in view of the experience of the twentieth century, it is 'rational' to accept in considering the forces of 'non-reason'.

Let me make clear what I am getting at by considering a statement Professor Peters makes regarding young people. He urges that to use authority 'is an immoral way to treat a child'; and he follows this up by defending young people against the crabbed comments of their elders on the grounds that 'What they often mean is that young people insist on thinking out their own principles'. And here, of course, we are brought up short. For, though this may be true of some—as it has always been—it is certainly not true of all. Many young people, instead of accepting the 'authority' of their parents, substitute blind obedience to the demands of the group, to the 'charismatic' influence of teen-age singing idols, to the tyranny of fashions dictated with an eye exclusively fixed on the financial profits, and so on. As the Crowther Report has it: '. . . all that has happened is the substitution of the public opinion of their peers for the wisdom of the ages.' However much we may regret the coming of Organization Man, we must grant that he provides something that Professor Peters' hard rational separateness does not—gregariousness, warmth and togetherness and all sorts of irrational things of that sort. And I cannot help thinking that too often Dr. Peters' notion of respect for others involves leaving them alone in indifference.

What is revealed by this phenomenon—what indeed is implicit also in *Wuthering Heights*—is a power of affective life at work in the human personality which Dr. Peters' brand of rationalism barely touches. Professor Peters is right to insist that fundamentally Freud was a rationalist; but he was a rationalist who realized the enormous power of the affective life ('the unconscious is the true psychic reality') and who in any case was concerned with the reassertion of the force of the rational ego only in cases where that affective life was out of control. In this process, the 'transference' was an essential aspect of the cure: in other words, he considered some sort of emotional outlet as an essential element in the right ordering of the emotional life.

Where learning is concerned, it is often the emotion generated through the personality of the teacher which sparks off an enthusiasm and which, therefore, first engages the attention of the learner. The discovery that interest is of great importance in learning leads us on to appreciate that that interest can be aroused by a mode of presentation, and that an essential part of some such mode springs out of the clash of personality on personality, a clash, of course, which needs to be controlled in terms of the subject-matter in hand. In the teaching of literature, for instance, I would not consider that a suggestion made a few years ago concerning a large supply of books and no teaching provided an ideal solution to the problem; for it is on the teacher's capacity to convey through his reading aloud, to light up what is to the modern child a strange and unusual mode of expression, that much of the success of the enterprise depends. And here the teacher needs to demand an attention, to impose a hearing so as to banish a thousand other fugitive echoes which, in the world outside school, mock at his efforts; not to mention the right he has which stems from a profounder understanding. Nor need he be denied the right lest the child should have no opportunity to make up his own mind; there is no point in making up one's mind in ignorance of the stakes at issue.[1]

In terms of such categories of experience, controlled, that is, by the material in hand and not simply springing out of a desire for power, the teacher, I think, has a right to make demands, to interpose a charismatic element. I remember hearing

---

[1] It may be urged that there is a difference between demanding an attention and imposing a view-point. The teacher may say: 'You must listen to this'—he may not add: 'and you must accept or like it.' True; but we may surely use more vitally suasive efforts than simply a flat, impersonal presentation of something we know to be good to make it acceptable to immature judges. That the legitimate boundaries of such suasion are difficult to draw provides no excuse for not seeing the need.

The Rôle of the Teacher

Sir John Gielgud tell how Granville Barker's driving, rigidly demanding methods in production evoked a response from him of which he did not consider himself capable. Ernest Jones reported on Freud's 'awe' for Brücke and told how, when in later life Freud was tempted to shirk his work, Brücke's terrible eyes would haunt him. Many of the great teachers have worked in this, or similar, ways; the phenomenon of an enthusiasm caught, not from a situation, but from the dynamic effect of personality on personality, is so common a classroom experience that one is surprised at Professor Peters' distrust.

When Professor Peters rejects an authority which is purely mechanical or which springs purely from a desire for power, I am with him all along the line; when he fails to note the tremendous creative effort that can be inspired by a use of authority such as I have alluded to, I feel he has failed to learn a lesson of the twentieth century. His abstract man is an Edgar Linton in a Cathy-Heathcliff triangle. That some of our experience with 'strong' personalities in the twentieth century has been unfortunate is no excuse for not seeing, rationally, if you like, from whence their power sprang; and that the harnessing of this power of the affective life for good is the twentieth century challenge in a world which leaves so many people an easy prey to the wrong affective influences. Two of the most widespread manifestations of our day are a pervasive cynicism and an adulation for the cheap, the meretricious—two sides of the same coin. Professor Peters' moral claim for moral neutrality springs from sources which are decent and respect-worthy, but it has too little relevance to an age when so many young people seek, not 'sweet reason', but that which has an element of the charismatic[1] in it—and find it in such undesirable places.

The job of the teacher then, seems to me to warrant a wider range of behaviour and procedures than our progressives are

---

[1] Just as in religious terms, 'charisma' indicates 'grace', something bestowed on the personality from outside—so that Christ becomes not only Himself as Man but representative of the Father also—so the 'charismatic' teacher has bestowed on him a secular 'grace' derived from the discipline he represents.

always willing to grant. I have stressed that the educative situation is inevitably one involving moral values. Whatever is done is done because the teacher decides to do it—he can escape neither the consequences of passivity nor those of interference. His behaviour indeed may tend to vary in accordance with how he relates the positive benefits of learning in contrast to the negative virtues of 'freedom from'. But those who accept a view of 'rational' freedom[1] will see nothing incongruous in admitting the power to bind—to spell-bind, if possible—as an admissible part of the teacher's practice. This does not reflect on the precise technique followed—which will follow from the nature of the discipline; but, however free the situation may seem to be within which the child is to learn, the very intensity with which he follows his own self-activity within the experimental framework will in part depend on the implicit or explicit expectations he infers from his teachers.

Finally, in the current concern for 'learning-motivation', it is well to remember that one traditional motivation was teacher expectation—theoretically out of date, no doubt, and certainly liable to abuse, but perhaps worth more consideration than some educationists normally give it?

[1] The phrase is taken from Mr. Maurice Cranston's *Freedom: A New Analysis*.

7

T. S. Eliot and Education

It is the difference of perspective which makes Eliot's comments on education so valuable. Current theorizing in, and discussion of, education are considerably taken up with problems relating to class, social justice and the economy—the three areas of concern are, in some degree, inter-related. Basically, our thinking about education is dominated by political necessities and social policy. Eliot's concern arose out of a different set of priorities; he sees education as a cultural manifestation and seeks to define the part it can play in a healthy cultural order. His slant of attention is partly explicable in terms of the nature of his own enterprises. The creative effort implicit in the writing of poetry and criticism and the particular view of human experience such writing involved made him suspicious of socio-political abstractions—Henry James, he reminds us, had so fine a mind it could never be violated by an idea. They did more. They brought home to him the accuracy of Matthew Arnold's diagnosis of the necessity of the moment to the man for the highest creative effort; they posed the problem of the educative rather than of the functional society.

Like other social thinkers, Eliot, in attempting to define the nature of his approved society, projected into its social relations the tensions and antinomies he found characteristic of his own deepest experience and which he expressed in his poetry. Informing his later writing, of course, is the antinomy of the Fall and the Redemption; but he was aware also of the timeless within time, the tensions of past and present, of end and beginning, of stillness and movement, of all those human attempts to make sense of present experience which nevertheless implied the logic of the past. He saw that at the heart of human destiny there was both conflict and tension and that any harmony achieved involved the uncertain and precarious resolution of opposites—a still point in a turning world; he appreciated that an abundant social life could not arise out of attempts at unilateral adjustment and harmony but involved, at best, precarious triumphs through momentary reconciliations and states of equilibrium:

> The danger of freedom is deliquescence; the danger of strict order is petrifaction.

An uncertain pathway through such antinomies was what man at most could seek; and yet, paradoxically, such tensions afforded in themselves creative opportunities. At the time when 'unity' and 'adjustment' have become increasingly the catchwords of our life in society, Eliot urged the creative importance of friction:

> Fortunate the man who, at the right moment, meets the right friend; fortunate also the man who at the right moment meets the right enemy.

The personal dilemma needed to be generalized into a universal 'irritation'; and this irritation should be institutionalized in terms of a diversity of classes and regional differences to maintain a proper balance between rigidity and fluidity; even the relations between the secular and the ecclesiastical should involve a degree of conflict as well as of co-operation. These are some of

> an indefinite number of conflicts and jealousies which would be profitable to society. Indeed, the more the better, so that everyone should be an ally of everyone else in some respects, and no one conflict, envy or fear will dominate.

In an age of social engineering, these views, of course, are eccentric; a pervasive aim today is precisely at the elimination of conflict. Similarly, Eliot's profound historical sense is at odds with current concern about the future rather than the past. His appreciation of the historical dimension to human experience

makes him sceptical of the larger claims made in the name of
social and political action. Certainly, he must not be associated with an inert conservatism: 'Tradition cannot mean stand-
ing still.' But he is too aware of the formative power of historical
circumstance, that 'Time present and time past' have their
part in 'time future', that a lifetime is 'burning in every moment', to be easily persuaded that, for instance, the value of the
formal education society imposes is other than ambivalent. It
is true that if by education we imply an induction, an assimilation into a heritage, Eliot himself was essentially an educated
poet—educated, too, in a specifically academic sense; he could
easily have been a university don. Yet his view of the poet's
functioning, of that extinction of personality which he considered to be an essential concomitant of the writing of poetry,
is perhaps a way of deprecating the element of *will*—rather than
of *willingness* derived from habit, breeding and environment,
which he considers to be the true sources of tradition—which
is necessarily involved in all forms of state action, including
formal education.

His more specific comments on education, indeed, can be seen
to involve the realization that culture is not something which
can be deliberately produced; it is something which arises as a
by-product of other activities: it is 'the one thing we cannot
deliberately aim at':

> It is the product of a variety of more or less harmonious
> activities, each pursued for its own sake; the artist must con-
> centrate upon his canvas, the poet upon his typewriter, the
> civil servant upon the just settlement of particular problems as
> they present themselves upon his desk, each according to the
> situation in which he finds himself.

The process, like that involved in the writing of poetry,
necessitates a degree of 'impersonality', a passive attending
upon the event. In so far as modern education becomes a
conscious device for the attainment of desirable social states of
being, the wished-for consummation of our educational policy
is likely, to that extent, to elude our grasp. Education, as Eliot
himself points out, becomes itself an abstraction imposed for

purposes in large measure irrelevant to its nature, instead of being simply a desirable concomitant to specific social functionings. In the past education of varying types has been *sought* or just accepted because it was the unself-conscious accompaniment of specific social and vocational rôles—whether of 'gentleman' or of craftsman. Today education is *imposed* for the attainment of abstract social ends remote, in large measure, from specific social relationships and neighbourhood demands and rôles. It is a means, not to integration and confirmation of status, but to mobility and dispersal. As such it serves the interests of a comparatively few who can benefit from its nature but, as at present constituted, is largely meaningless in the lives of the many.

It was Eliot's supreme virtue that, in essence, he saw the implications of this. He realized that formal education can, at best, from its very nature, play only a restricted part in the lives of the people; the schools can only transmit a part of a culture, and they can only do this effectively if

> the outside influences, not only of family and environment, but of work and play, of newsprint and spectacles and entertainment and sport, are in harmony with them.

This insight, at a time when the most absurd claims are being made for education, comes as an immense relief. But he goes further; formal education cannot itself create or save a culture because it is itself one of the instruments through which the culture manifests itself. Above all, however, he stresses that because modern education is an abstraction—in past times people had the 'education necessary for the functions they were called upon to perform'—it implies a disintegrated society

> in which it has come to be assumed that there must be one measure of education according to which everyone is educated simply more or less.

What he is doing here is to give the lie to Matthew Arnold's notion that 'the men of culture are the true apostles of equality'. The notion of a common culture, which is implicit in Arnold's statement (it is, of course, to be *his* culture, the irrelevance of

which to the interests and capacities of the traditional folk
Arnold failed to see), is one which has exercised a certain
influence on current educational theorizing; it accords with the
egalitarian tendencies of the day. Implicit in our view of education since the Act of 1876 finally imposed literacy on a total
population has been the notion that we must try to impose
the same culture on all classes. The bankruptcy of this policy is
everywhere apparent in the almost total ineffectiveness of the
culture of the schools in face of the culture of the mass media,
which has become the true, if debased, folk culture of our times.
Eliot has been one of the very few to diagnose the error involved:

> Error creeps in again and again through our tendency to
> think of culture as group culture exclusively, the culture of the
> 'cultured' classes and élites. We then proceed to think of the
> humbler part of society as having culture only in so far as it
> participates in this superior and more conscious culture. To
> treat the 'uneducated' mass of the population as we might treat
> some innocent tribe of savages to whom we are impelled to
> deliver the true faith, is to encourage them to neglect or despise
> that culture which they should possess and from which the more
> conscious part of culture draws vitality; and to aim to make
> everyone share in the appreciation of the fruits of the more
> conscious part of culture is to adulterate and cheapen what you
> give.

He sees not only that school culture has little relevance to the
lives of the bulk of the people; he appreciates also that the
attempt to disseminate what is essentially minority culture will,
in the end, destroy, or at least adulterate, such culture—an
appreciation for which there is already a certain amount of
evidence:

> For it is an essential condition of the preservation of the
> quality of the culture of the minority, that it should continue to
> be a minority culture.

Yet, by implication, he has to admit that the conditions for
the preservation of such minority culture no longer fully exist.
As I have urged, Eliot realizes that a culture grows as much out

of an unconscious assimilation as out of a conscious striving. A peculiar characteristic of our times lies in its belief that more and more areas of our behaviour and understanding should be brought to consciousness; and this, as Eliot accurately diagnoses, 'is a very great strain'. Part of his objection to Liberalism arises out of the way in which it destroys 'traditional social habits of the people' and 'dissolves their natural collective consciousness into individual constituents'. Such a process, of course, is peculiarly characteristic of a too rapid social mobility (such as we witness at the moment) and the substitution of élites based on intellectual ability for a traditional aristocracy leavened by the assimilation of the outstandingly able. In this way, continuity of consciousness is lost—a continuity which required the nurture of family and neighbourhood life as well as a conscious passing on through education; and family life, it should be noted, implies a 'piety towards the dead, however obscure, and a solicitude towards the unborn, however remote'. An élite comes together largely on the grounds of intellectual success unleavened by any similarity of background assumption; such a group will lack social cohesion and social continuity:

> They will be united by a part, and that the most conscious part, of their personalities; they will meet like committees.

It is essential to realize that Eliot's educational thinking does not involve a defence of aristocracy but an attempt to define the conditions of cultural health in a true democracy. On this he himself explicitly insists: he has in mind the total cultural health of our society so that each section of the community shall be afforded that opportunity for fulfilment of which it is capable. His work has been ignored because our concern is with narrowly conceived political rights rather than with the total range of satisfactions open to the people. 'Equality of opportunity' has come to be interpreted in terms of an opportunity for personal advancement rather than of one for personal fulfilment. Of course, there are times when the one will encompass the other —advancement and fulfilment will meet. But there are many occasions when some degree of incompatibility between the two will be involved; and there are many for whom advancement does not exist. In any case, even advancement will be the richer for the fuller life that an adequate culture can provide.

I persist in finding *Notes towards the Definition of Culture* (supplemented by a number of Eliot's other educational writings) one of the few fundamental educational treatises of our times because it stimulates to a profounder diagnosis of our education ills than is implicit in any of the official attempts to adumbrate a policy for schools and universities.

8

Considerations of Quality

When Matthew Arnold went to examine the system of education in Switzerland, he became critical of certain features of
Swiss democracy. It was, he said 'socialistic, in the sense in
which that word expresses a principle hostile to the interests of
true society—*the elimination of superiorities*'.

Arnold's criticisms of the aristocracy of his day are notorious
and largely justified; yet, he recognized that, in the past,
such an aristocracy had been in the 'grand style', and had set
the people an 'invaluable example of qualities without which
no really high welfare can exist'.

As our social life has become more egalitarian, the problem of
quality has been posed with ever increasing force. What happens when the notion of standards—call it 'superiority' or
noblesse—ceases to be institutionalized? However inadequately, in
practice, the superior class may live up to its pretensions, it yet
affords some degree of actuality to ideas of nobility, of courtesy,
of *arete*: at the very least, it keeps alive the notion of differentiation. When such views of 'superiority' cease to have any concrete manifestation within the social structure, how is qualitative
differentiation to be maintained? This is the problem that
begins to haunt us as the unstable élitism of the market has
gradually come to replace the continuities implicit in birth and
inheritance. For now artists and writers depend on the vagaries
of public taste rather than on private patronage.

The American response to the situation has been the
philosophy of pragmatism and the attempt to deny any hierarchy of values—among school subjects, for instance, as in the

case of John Dewey; 'We cannot,' he says, 'establish a hierarchy of values among studies.'[1] The consequences of this have become manifest in America itself. In *The Observer* colour supplement recently, Mr. Lee Minoff trumpeted the virtues of the University of Texas, where 'more than twenty-five senior professors earn $25,000 a year, including the thirty-nine year old football coach who, after leading the Longhorns to the national championship in 1963, was made a full professor with life tenure'. And he observes, without a hint of irony: 'There is little doubt that the University of Texas is bent on Total Distinction.'

The incident is significant, partly because it indicates how hard it is to resist or avoid qualitative considerations (of a sort); and yet the whole article also reveals a startling lack of qualitative distinction within the qualitative judgments which are made. The impulse remains—Texas has the most manuscripts, the best coiffured girls, the highest paid professors, all equally representative of 'Total Distinction'. If the reaction of the English don to such indiscriminate offerings is likely to be derisory, it is because, in general, he has assimilated a tradition which still asserts—with, perhaps, increasing lack of conviction—the superiority of the things of the mind over the externals of bodily appearance and success in competitive enterprises.

The 'culture' implicit, for instance, in Dr. Leavis's minority culture, which represents a classic formulation within the modern period of an important tradition of English discrimination, is one based on literacy and the consciousness and inwardness which a sophisticated literacy can develop; and Dr. Leavis's highly self-conscious notion of culture stretches back in time to Coleridge's 'possessors of ideas' and Arnold's 'small circle apt for fine distinctions'; back to the time, indeed, when the market and what it implied were beginning to displace the aristocratic patron as the major source of approval and the traditional defenders of culture began to lack institutionalized recognition.

[1] Though, of course, in the long run he can't avoid doing so, as Dr. F. W. Garforth points out in his Introduction to a recent compilation of extracts of Dewey's thought.

Considerations of Quality

So, the 'nobility' implicit in the (idealized) behaviour of certain recognizable social groups is replaced during the nineteenth and twentieth centuries by the abstract and disembodied superiority implied in such notions as the 'finer consciousness', a 'refined sensibility', 'maturity'. Dr. Leavis, indeed, offers no general view of sustaining social structure, as, for instance, his contemporary, Eliot, does. The 'continuity' he appeals to is essentially a continuity of minds, nurtured especially, though not exclusively, on literature and springing from any section of the community capable of the necessary 'responses'.

Dr. Leavis is not really interested in the structure of society; he simply assumes a selective process within a meritocratic élite—a minority within a minority, indeed, for he is as critical of some highly differentiated academic coteries and of a minority group like Bloomsbury as he is of mass civilization. 'Superiority', for him, arises out of qualitative distinctions made within an accepted discipline, that of literature—distinctions for which the evidence must be produced and which allow the democratic right implicit in the projected come-back: 'This is so, isn't it?' He posits, in other words, an essentially open society. Yet such a qualitative minority as Dr. Leavis defines is almost unknown to the mass audience, is under hostile attack from the other rejected minorities (academic reactions to Dr. Leavis are often violent), and, thus, leads a socially precarious existence. It is not, perhaps, totally without social influence, though such influence as it possesses arises out of the accidents of personal prestige rather than out of any assumed position within the community. The nearest such a minority approaches to achieving an institutional status is as an academic community, a university—and that largely an idealized one: 'we . . . knew we were . . . the essential Cambridge', as Leavis said in his attack on Snow. Yet I can't help thinking that Dr. Leavis's conception of a minority represents very nearly the actual position of superiorities within a democratic order and makes T. S. Eliot's notion of a superior class as being necessary to the adequate transmission of culture seem idealistic and remote.

158

But Eliot does add something. He asserts, indeed, the need for continuity through socially stable groups within the community. And his insistence on such hereditary continuity—implicit in a class—as well as on one of consciousness—implicit in an élite—contains an important insight. For this notion of class, with its seeming irrelevance amid today's fluidities, is, in fact, a means of introducing a stern reality into the debate which we ignore at our peril.

Eliot regarded the *Notes towards the Definition of Culture* as an important part of his life's work; and he was not so unrealistic in it as his critics have often asserted. For his insistence on the hereditary element is a means of stressing the relevance of tradition, of history, of continuity; and he wanted to stress these because he realized a truth we mostly neglect; that social forms, institutions and individuals have all arisen out of historical circumstances which present formidable obstacles to change —and that, all too often, mock at those changes we do engineer. Eliot was intensely aware of the influence of the family, of the intimate, half conscious and half unconscious assimilation which goes to form the depths of the consciousness of the growing child, on whom the influences of a formal, largely cognitive education devoted to the idea of changing him must, in the nature of things, be limited.

This insight, that the future must necessarily be impregnated with the spirit of the past, adds a social dimension to our thinking about qualitative transmission; it enters a protest against excessive mobility—but it is one so unpalatable that it is generally ignored. We assume, all too easily, the infinite possibilities of social engineering. It is, perhaps, for this reason that Eliot's influence on education has been so slight. Dr. Leavis's has been greater; for he introduces no checks to promulgation, no hereditary element. He requires the debate, within limits, to remain open—indeed, some of his lesser disciples introduce a revivalist note, an attempt at large scale conversion. If only we could persuade more people to read the right novels and plays, even the right newspapers, the minority *might* become a majority. The difference between the two men comes out, too, in the matter of style; Dr. Leavis's convoluted enthusiasm against Eliot's cooler tone. Leavis's very intransigence also helps, the feeling of an embattled and aggressive minority, the teacher as missionary.

Yet, in general, the aggression is against other minorities; where 'mass civilization' is concerned, the attitude is more one of defensive resistance. 'All that can be done, it must be realized,' as Mr. Leavis has said, 'must take the form of resistance by an armed and conscious minority.' And, although the actual critical practice has led to the defining of a very positive tradition of English writing and this belies any charge of negativism, the notion of 'minority culture' has proved insufficiently accommodating and flexible to please some of those who, like Mr. Raymond Williams, have a certain respect for the qualitative concern it implied. What irks about the idea is defined by Mr. Williams as a 'damaging arrogance and scepticism', a 'pseudoaristocratic authoritarianism'.

The appearance on the scene of essentially minority figures whose roots are yet self-consciously in the working classes—I have people like Williams and Professor Richard Hoggart in mind—takes the debate an important stage further. To my mind, their attempt to reconcile two basically incompatible loyalties, one to the qualitative considerations implicit in the minority idea and the other to the majority group whose own positive qualitative contribution has been minimal within the industrial period, partly fails. It leads them to overstress the contribution that ordinary people can make to the sustaining of our culture. But it does have one important repercussion. Their loyalty to their childhood origins—the group cohesiveness of working class life awakens a strong nostalgia in those who have been born into it—enables them to assess more accurately the notion of mass civilization and to differentiate more carefully within it. As Raymond Williams puts it: 'I do not think of my relatives, friends, neighbours, colleague acquaintances, as masses; we none of us can or do. The masses are always the others, whom we don't know, and can't know. . . . There are in fact no masses; there are only ways of seeing people as masses.'

Considerations of Quality

This is well said, for it points, among other things, to the error of equating a particular manifestation of quality within a specific minority group with the total (cultural) health of the community. Two points can be made here; one is that the health of the minority culture is itself dependent on the cultural health of the whole community and, therefore, cannot be divorced from the problem of mass civilization. The other is that the culture of literacy is only one sort of *culture* (albeit a most important one because of the rôle that words and language play in our common life). For our civilization, which has developed, partly through technical means, a wide variety of cultural forms, contains a tremendous variety of opportunity for qualitative differentiation.

The error which equates the whole culture with the culture of the lettered is one perhaps natural in a civilization which has so recently imposed literacy on a total population—a quite extraordinary demand in the history of mankind. Paradoxically, it may be the spread of education as we conceive it, institutionalized and based for the most part on a variety of verbal forms of sophistication (humanistic and scientific), that has contributed to the current crisis in our culture. The rapid growth of the reading public, which goes on all during the nineteenth century, coincides with the break-down of the cultural forms dependent on an agricultural order of society and the means of production relevant to it, with their wider opportunities for creative work (a variety of crafts) arising out of daily labour. The expansion of the market manifests a *qualitative* change in which the *quantifiable* comes increasingly to count; and the traditionally debased reading habits of considerable sections of the population (which comprised chapbooks and other, inferior literary forms) comes to achieve, in our own times, a prominence and an opportunity for profit which arouses the worst fears of those who cannot see the education of the bulk of the people in other than literary terms.

The problem of quality today arises, in part at least, because a social necessity has become a cultural embarrassment; a verbal sophistication beyond their scope is demanded of people who, traditionally, have expressed themselves culturally in a variety of other forms more amenable to the particular nature of their talents. The need to write, especially, imposes considerable psychic strains on those who, in the past, have been satisfied with oral communication (often of a limited nature) and in whose historical consciousness little need for written communication has arisen.

It is, it seems to me, when we come to see people, not as a mass public for the largely (though, of course, by no means exclusively) decreative media of mass communication, but as pigeon fanciers, market gardeners, riders of horses, amateur singers and actors, photographers and cine enthusiasts, and so on, that the qualitative opportunities open to a modern community set the problem of mass civilization in a rather different perspective. 'Culture', in fact, is what happens when people pursue activities with passion and discrimination. Not that anyone should fall into the error of rating these various forms of activity as of equal value, but that each should offer its creative possibilities within what seems a neutralized or debased cultural situation. In the same way, we need to make discriminations *within* what is being presented through the mass media themselves.

Here lies the importance of *The Popular Arts* by Stuart Hall and Paddy Whannell. Whatever shortcomings such a book may have, it introduces the analytical procedure in a sphere where it has, in general, been lacking (with the exception of Orwell's work) and offers a number of particularized judgments in the Leavisian spirit ('That is so, isn't it?') within the field of mass civilization itself. Though most of mass culture can be dismissed as uncreative and deadening, qualitative discrimination reveals some genuine features. Who will deny the greatness of Chaplin, for instance?

The situation is, perhaps, being further complicated by the social scientists. In general, the concern for standards has been in the hands of literary people; and this concern has been manifest largely in terms of content analysis, with extrapolations regarding possible effects based on such analysis.

Considerations of Quality

Now, however, there is a growing attempt to *measure* and assess the influence of particular manifestations on different types of personality: the same programme or subject-matter may have quite different effects on different people. The predispositions of the individual are important and what is seen or heard is subject to a number of mediating factors which may effectively filter the original content, in some cases to the point of unrecognizability; an extreme example would be—an actual case —the adolescent girl who made Lydia Bennett into the heroine of *Pride and Prejudice* because Lydia's particular forms of irresponsibility tied in with the girl's own adolescent desires for erotic adventure and escape. The mistaken interpretation of the book is an indication that from content analysis it cannot necessarily be assumed that the content has been received as intended. At the same time, the social scientist's own assessment as to what is implicit in the matter under review often needs the trained guidance that a highly skilled literary critic, or any other sort of critic practised in the interpretation of any form or level of imaginative content, can offer.

The entry of the social scientist into prominence in our society may prove a complicating factor in other respects. For the debate continues within the sophisticated minority also, of which the sociologist is a member. His growing social prestige encourages a value-free approach; qualitative judgments become inhibited. Responses to aspects of the mass media, diagnosed, imply social phenomena of an interesting nature; but it is not our job, the social scientist implies, to evaluate such responses. Of course, he is right where he himself is concerned; social *science* involves the analysis of what *is*. But others shelter behind this curtain of neutrality for less reputable reasons.

On the one hand, neutrality is the financially interested reaction of the advertising agent, who employs social science techniques, but whose interests are bound up with quantitative rather than qualitative responses. On the other, there are those who make a virtue of indifference to qualitative considerations on the grounds, partly, that the charge of mass corruption through the media is not proven in strictly measurable terms, and, partly, because such an attitude of neutrality enables them to adopt an appearance of liberality which accords well with the permissive morality of the day. This is, naturally, all grist to the mill of the self-indulgent, among whom any hint of moral evaluation relevant to their activities is likely to evoke the charge of 'Puritanism'.

For what is becoming apparent—and it is confirmed by a recent article in *New Society*—is that those who, in terms of ability, seem to constitute the minority element in the community are, in fact, being increasingly influenced by exposure to mass cultural forms. Thus, Harold L. Wilensky, in 'High Culture and Mass Culture' (14th May, 1964) shows the extent to which even the highly educated participate in mass cultural activities: 'Intellectuals are increasingly tempted to play to mass audiences and expose themselves to mass culture, and this has the effect of reducing their versatility of taste and opinion, their subtlety of expression and feeling.'

Out of a cross-section of 1,354 members of the community only nineteen could be found who had made 'rather heroic efforts to cultivate the best in the media'—and most of these were university professors.[1] In general, these nineteen had 'inherited higher occupational status than their colleagues (their parents tended to be established professionals and executives)—which suggests that it may take rather close family supervision over more than a generation to inculcate a taste for high culture'—a conclusion which, uncomfortably, bears out T. S. Eliot's thesis.

In some respects, then, the debate is more open; the notion of mass civilization has, itself, undergone an evaluation. Yet the attempt to impose, through education, a watered-down version of 'high culture' may have contributed to the process of mediocratisation which remains one of the most insistent impressions received of the current situation. There has, perhaps, been both a levelling-up, through education, and a levelling-down, through

[1] This has to be born in mind when we are tempted to place too much reliance on the cultural force of the school—the teachers themselves too often participate in mass culture in a quite undiscriminating way.

the market education has provided for inferior cultural goods. The state of even our 'high' culture today is such that one can only live in much of it as an ironic stranger. That is why the school and university, as the repositories of the past, have so crucial a rôle to play in keeping alive some memory of former standards.

1965

9

The Two Cultures: Can the Gap be Bridged?

The main thesis of Sir Charles Snow's famous Rede lecture is by now well known; it is that

> the intellectual life of the whole of western society is increasingly being split into two polar groups . . . at one pole we have the literary intellectuals . . . at the other scientists, and as the most representative, the physical scientists.

Some have denied that such a gulf exists; others have assumed its existence and have attempted to show ways by which the gap can, in some degree at least, be closed. I believe a gap does exist. But I do not feel it is possible to discuss the feasibility of its being bridged until we have analysed more closely what is involved in the notion of literary 'culture' and scientific 'culture'; and the most important feature of such an analysis is the examination of what is involved in the literary and scientific activities. For, indeed, my impression is that the discussion has been befogged by the fact the people have assumed that they have had a clear view in their heads as to what has been implied both by 'litera-ture' and by 'science' and that discussion as to the asserted polarity of the two groups can go ahead on this basis. My own opinion is that an enormous amount depends on precisely what is intended by 'literature' and by 'science' in the context of the discussion—especially, perhaps, what is meant by 'literature'; and that much of one's awareness or otherwise of the gap which

The Two Cultures: Can the Gap be Bridged?

is said to exist between the two will be bound up with what one has precisely in mind when one refers to the two areas of interest.

It should be obvious, in the first place, that activities which necessitate classifications under different headings are likely to show some difference of nature. I remember once having a long discussion with a scientist about the difference between science and literature. I urged a number of general characteristics which I thought applied to literature—involving, for instance, imagination, subjectivity, and so on. On each occasion my comments were capped by the statement that such categories applied equally to the nature of science. In the end, of course, what was happening was obvious. In no way could it be maintained that science and literature were the same sorts of activity; otherwise, there would be no analysable difference between what emerged as science and what came out as literature, and this is palpably and demonstrably not so; a set of scientific formulae does not read like a poem. What was at fault was the extraordinary poverty of our critical vocabulary, so that, in fact, very different activities had to be described by the same word. The sort of way in which imagination is used in science is obviously different from the sort of way in which it is used in literature. The word 'imagination,' in fact, can be used with reference to a whole range of human activities, from simple fantasy-living to that 'coalescence of subject and object' which marks the exercise of the imagination in the Coleridgean sense. To say, then, that both literature and the sciences employ the imagination is to say very little; everything depends on the precise activity to which the same word refers in the different contexts in which it is used.

But, once it is admitted that literature is not the same as science, it still remains to point out that literature moves nearer towards or further away from the scientific mode in accordance with the nature of the particular piece of literature which is at hand. For it is important to realize that the word 'literature,' in a fairly loose usage but implying some pretensions to quality, covers a whole range of writing of very different degrees of wroughtness and intensity. In the reasonably evaluative sense in which I am employing it we would have to include such very different sorts of writing as the prose works of Swift, with their controlled prosaic intensity, the incredibly metaphorical later plays of Shakespeare—and the novels of Trollope and of Sir Charles Snow himself. One has only to think even of a set of writers like the Romantics who, although they go under a common label, nevertheless include writings as different as those of the highly coloured intenseness of Keats, the sober ruminative Wordsworth or the aristocratic insolence of Byron to appreciate the differences of intensity covered by the same label. And over the field of literature as a whole, the range is enormous.

Something of the same sort, of course, is true of the sciences, especially if the social sciences are included. The social sciences have tried to ape the natural sciences in some of their manifestations; but, in so far as they have remained true to themselves, their relationship to literature has been that much the closer; they have needed to employ that imaginative and empathic projection into the minds of other people which is part of the literary man's equipment. Sir Charles, of course, is more concerned with the natural sciences; but, even here, scientists are agreed that there are significant differences in the exercise of the various sciences, though the scientific outlook is probably a more homogeneous manifestation than the literary one.

My point, then, is that the gap is not a constant one; Snow's metaphor about two opposite poles is to that extent false. The gap widens and narrows in accordance with the particular work of literature under review. Let me take as an example the novels of Sir Charles himself. The most obvious thing to be said about them is that one is not surprised to learn that they have been written by a scientist; they are, in fact, precisely the sort of novels one would expect a scientist to write, if he could write novels at all. They are, that is to say, essentially prosaic in character, involving only a telling about, never a presentation; this, I take it, is what Dr. Leavis is concerned about when he complains, in his Richmond lecture, that Snow tells you what you are to take him as doing, but he can give you no more than the telling. When the characters are supposed to fall in love you are told they do, but he can't show it happen . . . He announces in his chapter-headings the themes and developments in which we are to see the significance of what follows, but what follows adds nothing to the effect of the announcement . . .

These must be taken as the strictures of a critic who has announced comments on the novels he considers to be supreme of their kind under the general title of 'the novel as dramatic poem'. And it is in relation to the standard of presentation implicit in such a phrase that Leavis finds Snow to be wanting.

The fact of the matter is that such novels as Leavis has in mind—say those of Henry James or Lawrence—involve a quite different level of reading and attention from that demanded by the Snow writings; and the same would be true of all the most highly significant poetry and drama (though such significant writings need not be regarded as being co-extensive with what constitutes 'literature'). The ability to read such works demands not only a local sensitiveness to metaphor and imagery; it depends also on an ability to bring into significant relationship disparate parts of the novel or poem so that its inner coherence becomes clear; and this through a peculiar sensitivity to language and rhythm which is a matter of feeling as well as of intelligence. Thus what takes place in the reading is not only conscious intellectual response but half unconscious empathic projection, an ability to feel into the situation in hand. As Eliot put it—and his way of expressing it provides an alternative way of bringing out the significance of my point: 'The poet who "thinks" is merely the poet who can express the emotional equivalent of thought.'

The nature of responding to such works, then, is a matter of carefully controlled intellectual emotion; and the business of teaching how to read such works is a matter of developing this curiously complex mode of sensibility which neither aridly schematises the work under consideration nor responds as an outpouring of gush. Such a training is long and arduous and few

169

achieve the balancing of intellectual and emotional forces which is needed for its perfection. The same is true from the creative end; the penalties of failing to live up to this standard are to be found in the restricted emotional interest of the work of Snow or, conversely, in the false emotionality of a Dylan Thomas.

My point about all this is that any thought which must be given to the question as to how we can 'bridge the gap' must stem from an appreciation of what, more precisely, is involved in the gap. The important thing about science, it seems to me, from the point of view of the literary man is not that it leads to materialism so much as that it has tended to reduce what I will call the density of experience. For one thing, it is not so much that there is no emotion involved in scientific discovery as the fact that emotion is irrelevant in the actual schematic and explanatory constructions which the scientist produces. But, more important, the general effect of scientific discovery is to reduce the world to a set of abstractions in accordance with the nature and conventions of the scientific discipline which is being explored. As Gerard Manley Hopkins, who was himself a writer intensely interested in science, put it:

> The study of physical science has, unless corrected in some way, an effect the very opposite of what one would suppose. One would think it might materialize people . . . but in fact they seem to end in conceiving only of a world of formulas, with its being properly speaking in thought . . .

It is not only a matter of reducing the world to these sorts of abstractions, however; it is also a question of the fact that, insensibly, our scientific way of looking at things tends to make us regard the everyday world under a particular guise. We have come to accept, almost as second nature, certain sorts of explanation of phenomena, the general tendency of which is to explain them away and thus to make them seem of less importance, to deprive them particularly of an emotional dimension. To turn phenomena into 'natural' phenomena is to make them seem 'natural' in more than one sense. To take an obvious example, thunder and lightning have lost much of their awesome and magical quality which they undoubtedly possessed for pre-scientific man. Such manifestations inevitably shed a whole range of symbolic and mythical associations which reduces the possible range of interest such phenomena might have in ordinary experience and thus deprives the poet (and, indeed, the painter as well) of much of the *felt* experience which was open to his ancestors. To some extent this may be an explanation of much of that sort of cerebration which seems to characterize modernistic poetry—the strained metaphors, the consciously ratiocinated resemblances; or the degree of abstraction which characterises so much of modern painting, as if the real world no longer offered shapes which were sufficiently emotionally potent.

Now, what I am trying to suggest by this is that, at the higher levels of literary creativity, the antagonism which has seemed to exist between literary intellectual and scientist is based on a very real manifestation. Basically, the two modes of comprehension are, in some degree at least, mutually incompatible. Not only have scientific explanations, since the eighteenth century, appeared to have a prestige of 'truth,' of 'reality'—a prestige as yet unaffected in the lay mind by recent sophistications in the scientist's view of his job; the whole temper of mind—the analysis of phenomena—which science encourages makes it the more difficult to take the world 'feelingly,' as it were. The result has been an increasing intellectualization of one's view of the world—including the people in it—and a coarsening of feeling as the emotions have sought their outlet in the popular culture of the day.

It would, indeed, seem reasonable that the great writers, like Yeats and Lawrence, who have protested against the power of science should have intuitively realized that in some degree science has been destroying their world. And this is not only a protest against the element of will to power which is inherent in technology; it also stems from an appreciation of the peculiar nature of science and of its ability to cramp and confine their mode of appreciating their experience. Sir Charles's impatience with them, indeed, is grossly unfair. And he is unfair because it is clear from the sorts of novels he writes and the critical comments on literature that he makes, that, in fact, he has no real understanding of what the writing of literature in any deep sense necessitates. And it is when the standard of what we take to constitute literature refers to this sort of literature that we can come to see that the bridging of the gap is a much more difficult enterprise—if not, at the profoundest level, an impossible one—than it is commonly made out to be by the framers of educational syllabuses.

The nature of the difference can be approached through some words of Lawrence which are to be found in his *Fantasia of the Unconscious*: he speaks of a child:

> He will ask 'why' often enough. But he more often asks why the sun shines, or why men have moustaches, or why grass is green, than anything sensible. Most of a child's questions are, and should be, unanswerable. They are not questions at all. They are exclamations of wonder, they are *remarks* half-sceptically addressed. When a child says 'Why is the grass green?' he half implies, 'Is it really green, or is it just taking me in?' And we solemnly begin to prate about chlorophyll. Oh, imbeciles, idiots, inexcusable owls.

What are involved are two quite different approaches to the world. The one seems to 'explain' the phenomenon concerned; the other accepts it and responds to it for what it is in itself without, in Keats's phrase, 'any irritable reaching after fact and reason'. Of course, this is not the whole story in either case; indeed, such stories are in both cases immensely complicated ones, and, as I have indicated, they are stories that move nearer together or farther apart in accordance with the nature of the particular tale in hand. Furthermore, 'accept' is not completely the operative word; poetry is also a way of exploring and defining experience, but of exploring it 'feelingly,' as it were. When, for instance, Macbeth is contemplating the murder of Duncan, he could be said to be exploring the pros and cons of the situation, examining the arguments for and against the projected exploit; but what Shakespeare does is to give us his 'thoughts' embedded in the emotional state engendered by the tension in which Macbeth exists:

De Nicola

reserve

The Two Cultures: Can the Gap be Bridged?

> If it were done when 'tis done, then 'twere well
> It were done quickly; if the assassination
> Could trammel up the consequence and catch
> With his surcease success; that but this blow
> Might be the be-all and the end-all here,
> But here, upon this bank and shoal of time,
> We'd jump the life to come.

The movement of these lines marvellously reflects Macbeth's mental state. They begin slowly, hesitantly, the up and down movement and the close, clotted consonants, requiring a clenched jaw to speak them as they demand to be spoken, reflecting the tension that exists in Macbeth; the nervous strain of the situation is imposed upon us not only as a by-product of the weighing of possibilities that is going on but through the very enunciation of the arguments by which the experience is investigated.

To be sensitive to great literature, in fact, is to be sensitive to movement and rhythm—movement and rhythm as the very creation of the emotion and feeling implicit in the situation— at this level. As Dr. Leavis puts it:

> Words in poetry invite us, not to 'think about' and judge but to 'feel into' or 'become'—to realize a complex experience that is given in words (*The Common Pursuit*).

The emphasis must be on 'what the living thing feels like'; as Leavis brings out in his criticism of Samuel Johnson, works of art '*enact* their moral valuations'; they don't simply state them.

This, it seems to me, represents the central core of what a literary education must establish. There are, of course, other aspects; there is the bringing to consciousness for the purpose of discussion of one's awareness of significance in the work before one—the process that is particularly associated with Dr. Leavis, so that he is often accused, quite unjustifiably, of murdering to dissect. But this is no more than a process of making conscious what also exists at a profounder level of empathy and response and it is in no way a substitute for that prior, intuitive, grasp.[1]

[1] I have analysed the nature of Dr. Leavis's literary criticism in my *Education in an Industrial Society*.

The Two Cultures: Can the Gap be Bridged?

The central pedagogic problem in the teaching of literature, as I see it, lies here; and it is one to which, in essentials, the scientific approach is inimical. It is inimical because science must treat its objects of contemplation under that eye of severe intellectual abstraction of which I have already spoken, not as part of a complex of events which can be accepted in their full emotional significance. Indeed, the prime necessity for the scientist is to see them completely abstracted from any emotional connotation. The sort of training that an appreciation of literature requires is difficult enough without the barriers that such a state of affairs tends to set up. This is why 'Leavisian' analysis tends with so many to emerge as a set of 'tricks' which can be acquired intellectually by bright young men with a capacity for the subtler forms of stock response—a crime, of course, which should not be laid at the door of Dr. Leavis himself, for he has made the position quite clear and is innocent of the desire to turn out clever performing literary seals. This is why, in the early stages of a training in literature we ought to pay a great deal more attention than has been paid in the past to a *participation* in literature—I mean through drama, dance drama, choral speaking and, perhaps, mime and movement as well. The time when this participation should become more intellectualized—it will always need, to some extent, to be conscious, for 'participation' cannot simply be a matter of unconscious assimilation—needs to be carefully worked out; probably puberty is a good time, and then only for a limited section of the population.

This process is something other than a matter of bridging the gap by means of taking a few works of literature which exist as near to the scientific end of the spectrum as it is possible to discover; yet, in the last resort, it is the only satisfactory way of giving young people the experience of literature in a form which enables literature to 'work' in the way which is most true to its nature. I do not mean that the attempt to assimilate the two, in some degree, so that one starts as near to the mode of statement as possible, may not be helpful in getting the young scientist to read; what I do mean is that ultimately the experience of literature is not obtained until its subtler and more characteristic modes are explored.

I have said nothing about the scientific education of literary people. This is partly because this can only be conveniently handled by people a great deal more knowledgeable about the detailed facts of a science than I am. But there is a further reason; *pace* Sir Charles Snow, I still cannot help considering this the less pressing need. For the highly self-conscious, those who are intimately concerned to comment and reflect on the nature of their own experience, the fact that our way of looking at the world is so deeply influenced by scientific ways of regarding phenomena makes it necessary that such people should at least have some awareness of what is involved in the scientific outlook. For the rest, the comparatively unreflective, such understanding is largely irrelevant; their way of taking the world, as Lawrence pointed out, is largely 'symbolical, mythical, dynamic'; such people need the affective sustenance and the morality implicit in such knowledge; the technicalities of any advanced science is simply irrelevant to their needs.

II

When this chapter first appeared, Professor Paul Hirst carried on the debate in a very interesting article entitled 'The Two Cultures, Science and Moral Education'.[1] I would like to take up one or two remarks he has made there. He counsels caution to 'advocates of the importance of a literary education', for he thinks that in the Leavisian practice the moral element in literary judgments 'seems to be some form of intuition' without rational justification. Such intuitionism he finds 'notoriously unsatisfactory', for 'it is hard to escape the conclusion that . . . the intuitions are in fact the expression of previously held moral values that are being brought to the critical process'. If this is the case, the moral foundations in terms of which such judgments are being offered 'are going

---

[1] *Education for Teaching*, May, 1965.

unexamined and the education offered is then to say the least dangerously partial and uncritical.'

I am not clear as to how Professor Hirst arrives at the view that the moral element in literary judgments constitutes a form of 'intuitionism'. There are, it seems to me, two broad categories of judgment involved in what Professor Hirst refers to as literary judgment. There is the overall decision that this work of literature is good or bad or on some point on the scale between the two; and this will depend on a number of other judgments concerning the actual impact of the work. Where the work is finally adjudged to be 'good', it is certainly true that one of the possible effects of this impact will be, not to re-affirm previously held moral judgments, but to sensitize to the complexities and incompletenesses of such previously held views.

Let me illustrate with an example. Let us say that someone who holds that public duty should always take precedence over private interest were to read Shakespeare's *Antony and Cleopatra*. He would recognize his view put forward in the very first scene by a conventionally minded young Roman officer: of Antony, this young man says:

> . . . his captain's heart,
> Which in the scuffles of great fights hath burst
> The buckles on his breast, reneges all temper,
> And is become the bellows and the fan
> To cool a gipsy's lust.

The public soldier has yielded to private lusts. It is a clear cut case of the rigid application of moral categories.

But the rest of the play shows us that the issues are not so clear cut. For one thing, the world of public duty is not so morally refined as necessarily to invite an exclusive loyalty; it has, for instance, little care for individuals. 'They are worth the waste', says Caesar contemptuously of his men in ordering them some distribution of largesse after their victory; and the political world of the play is one of coarse personal ambitions as well as of some sense of political responsibility, of fickle popular opinion as well as of transcending loyalty. The world of private obligations involves positive fidelities (Eros, Enobarbus) as well as social and political irresponsibilities. Central to the conflict of forces is an ambivalence that sees Antony both as the 'strumpet's fool' and as that force of nature 'that grew the more by reaping'; crucial is the imagery of deliquescence, so

> That which is now a horse, even with a thought
> The rack dislimns, and makes it indistinct,
> As water is in water.

Similarly, moral categories themselves are blurred; and it is part of the essential quality of the play that they should be so. All that can be said is that anyone who came to such a play with a predetermined system of moral values must inevitably undergo some form of 'sea-change'; and that reorientation of moral rigidities forms an important part of the moral experience of great literature.[1]

[1] And let this truth remain as a comment even on my present work, with its emphasis on 'forms' and 'categories'. It's certainly these latter that need emphasis in modern educational discussion with its distaste for definition and clarity. But my analysis of *Antony* reminds me of the equivocation at the heart of 'formality' itself.

10

Culture and the University

The crisis in education today arises out of a crisis in consciousness. And, by this I mean a crisis in the *level* of consciousness and a crisis in the *range* of consciousness. The nature of this crisis has not, I think, been sufficiently realized by either Dr. Sloman in his recent Reith Lectures or by the authors of the Robbins Report.

Let me begin by explaining what I mean by *level* of consciousness. We are, today, asking a whole lot of people, who, in the past, have been largely governed in their daily lives by habit and tradition, to take more and more decisions about their lives at the level of conscious choice. To do this has meant that they have been asked to become increasingly *self*-conscious, to see themselves as separate units over against the other members of the community, with rights and responsibilities which require them to take personal decisions rather than to rely on traditional habits. This has led them to develop an atomic self to a degree which in the past has only been possible for a sophisticated élite. It has been necessary for the people referred to to become capable of some measure of abstraction and generalization. As a result, they have come to be more aware of connections and correlations, or, as Wordsworth puts it, of 'affinities. . . . In objects where no brotherhood exists. . . . To passive minds'. Furthermore, as some knowledge of, and liking for, the arts has spread from educated minorities to quite considerable numbers of people, much greater sophistications of feeling

178

have also been experienced by a larger section of the population than formerly.

This extension of consciousness has been purposely fostered by the proliferation of schools and colleges. The general purpose of these has been to diffuse by quite deliberate means consciously elaborated structures of 'knowledge' in order to convey the benefits of this 'minority' culture to as much of the community as possible. The crucial point here, however, is that what, in the culture of the minority, has been integrated in a whole way of life, and therefore has existed both at a conscious and at an unconscious level, becomes attenuated as it is formulated for the purpose of being passed on in this way. The first generation grammar school boy, for instance, often encounters a way of speaking and thinking which may be quite alien to the practices and prejudices of his home. He becomes de-rooted, and the smatterings of culture he receives are not supported by his life out of school.

Some parts of a culture, it is true, can be passed on more easily than others. That part, for instance, which employs an unequivocal vocabulary—such as science and mathematics—presents comparatively little difficulty in presentation, given the appropriate gifts for abstraction on the part of the student. But, where the language used—whether it be a matter of words, of musical notation or of handling paint—has its roots deep in the past of a culture, a past which contains both conscious and unconscious elements, it is not so easy to transmit. Poetry, for instance, arises out of the language of ordinary speech and carries with it the overtones and ambiguities of a language which has come to take on present meaning as a result of slow accretion rather than through arbitrary assignment.

This situation has had its effect on the other aspect of the current crisis in consciousness which I mentioned at the beginning —on, that is, the *range* of consciousness. For it has contributed to the overstimulation and, indeed, exploitation in the modern world of certain aspects only of our possible range of awareness. I can sum up what I have in mind by saying that what we tend to stress today are logico-empirical modes of thinking rather than creative-imaginative ones. Yet, a fully developed theory of mind will stress the need for the development of both aspects of consciousness. Discursive expression, as in science, is only one way in which we objectify the world around us; the construction of forms expressive of the emotional life in poetry, painting and music is equally important for human happiness. If psychological 'need' is to be one of the factors underlying our educational curriculum, then emotional factors require much more attention than they get at the moment.

There are profound repercussions for both the individual and the community in what I've said, which, so far as I can see, only T. S. Eliot, in his *Notes towards the Definition of Culture* has tried to diagnose. Briefly, these relate to the possible effects which the upward mobility of those without much cultural background—through the extension of university education, for instance—have on a culture. Eliot's pessimism in this respect may be unjustified; but, as the opinion of an especially learned poet and critic who is himself intensely aware of the discipline necessary for high achievement, it deserves at least the courtesy of consideration. Certainly, our culture contains unhealthy features; there is a lack of traditional counterpoise to the current instabilities of styles, there are uncertainties of audience which affect the artist. It must be stressed that the health of a culture has nothing to do with dilettantism, nor with *fin-de-siècle* aestheticism. A culture, properly conceived, embraces the ways in which we structure and communicate our common world—intellectually and emotionally. On this culture depends our ability to understand the world in its various guises; and from it stems the spiritual strength or weakness of a generation. Every single individual is involved in this.

I hope that what I have said so far indicates what should reasonably exercise the minds of those considering contemporary needs in education, particularly when, as with the Robbins Report, those needs concern the most highly educated group in the nation. I think that what I have described forms an essential part of the human predicament in an advanced industrial society which, by raising material standards of life, has brought along with it the cultural dilemmas to which I have referred. It is only in an economy of abundance, depending on scientific and technical advance, such as we are beginning to enjoy, that these dangers arise. A subsistence economy is normally underwritten by an unself-conscious traditionalism. This produces social inertness and thus inhibits the inwardness necessary for the development of self-consciousness. They have problems, too, but they are different ones.

Neither the Robbins Report nor Dr. Sloman in his Reith Lectures make any reference whatever to these vital matters. In so far as the Robbins committee was constituted in order to consider the whole *pattern* of higher education, and not just the universities, the need to analyse the cultural predicament in our society was, one would have thought, overwhelmingly imposed. Yet the absence of diagnoses in Robbins is amongst its most striking weaknesses; furthermore, it contains little more than a page and a half of discussion as to the purposes which the vast extension of higher education it recommends are to subserve— and a few vague gestures in the direction of new courses to be developed. Again, it omits to discuss areas of higher education one would have thought essential to a balanced society. There is, for instance, nothing on the colleges of music or drama, little on the colleges of art; the Report is concerned almost exclusively with cognitive education—and, vitally important though this is, it hardly provides a total pattern of higher education, and certainly not one fit to meet the crisis in consciousness which I have described.

The fact of the matter is that neither the members of the Robbins committee nor Dr. Sloman appear to be aware of cultural needs in the sense in which I have tried to define them here. Both, generously, have seen the need for a considerable expansion of higher education; but both have tended to see this need in terms of consumer demand, of professional need. They show little positive zeal for an education that would meet the deeper requirements of individuals living in a civilization faced with a problem of abundance, implying not only much more leisure in the near future but increased social mobility. In this sense the thinking of both is curiously old-fashioned. However much the Robbins committee may wish to avoid the imputation that their concern has been primarily economic, the fact of placing first among their aims 'instruction in skills suitable to play a part in the general division of labour' has, despite a subsequent retraction, exercised its subtle influence on their calculations and on the terminology they employ; so that there are frequent references to the need for a 'greatly increased stock of educated people', analogies between the 'production of trained manpower' and the 'production of long-lived capital goods', and emphasis on 'education as an investment'. And Dr. Sloman's consideration of national need has much the same ring about it. Here, the community service station idea of the university's rôle is even more explicit. One of his major considerations in the framing of a curriculum relates to the special features of the region: he refers to 'the leading industries of Essex with which we might be closely associated. Universities in this country, we believe', he goes on, 'should work much more closely with industry and with research institutions'. Dr. Sloman's praiseworthy salute to the arts—there is to be a centre for creative arts at Essex, though its nature is not yet very clear —only slightly off-sets the general impression he gives of subservience to business interests and professional requirements.

A remark by Dr. Sloman affords us a clue as to what may be thought wrong with this view of education. He urges the need for modernity, and lays stress on subjects 'relevant to the social, cultural and scientific realities of today'. Now, it may seem odd that, when I have already criticized his views as 'curiously old-fashioned', I should object to this stress on modernity; but, in fact, I believe his diagnoses of our current predicament to be inadequate and this because, in part, of his very desire to be in the van. Perhaps our conflict of views is in some respects analogous to that which existed between Plato and the Sophists. Both attempted to deal with the crisis of their times. The Sophists, in so far as one can lump them together, placed their emphasis on an entirely practical education, with particular concern, for instance, for rhetoric, which would enable the educated to play a prominent part in public life. Plato realized that the crisis involved something much more basic. This led him to ask fundamental questions about education and society. These, he saw, could only be tackled by attempting to find out the truth, in as far as it was humanly discoverable. Only when such an attempt had been made, did he think that the educated were fitted to apply their insights to day-by-day exigencies. Though his aim ultimately was action, Plato stands as a perpetual refutation of the explicit and implicit pragmatism of the Robbins committee and Dr. Sloman. There is a sense in which a concern for modernity can inhibit a proper assessment of the modern situation when the great classical writings which Dr. Sloman's university at Colchester is, it seems, largely to neglect, provide the basis for a truer disgnosis than some up-to-date calculation of the 'nation's needs'.

I am not, of course, arguing that the reasonable requirements of technical change should not be catered for; as Aristotle said: 'Those are clearly right who . . . maintain the necessity to a happy life of an addition in the form of material goods'. It is the extent to which what Lawrence stigmatized as the 'plausible ethics of productivity' has triumphed which is disturbing. For, among other things, to have so ready an excuse for the extension of higher education to hand has blinded the Robbins committee to the need for empirical assessments even more important than those they have undertaken. People like myself, who believe very much in the need for the extension of higher education, do not necessarily think that it should have come to the extent which it has in the universities. My own impressions as a teacher of graduate students for many years tally extremely well with those gained from recent books on higher education (such as Peret Marris's *The Experience of Higher Education*) where students have expressed some grave disappointment with what life at the university has meant to them. I would like, indeed, a survey to have been carried out concerning the actual results of a university education—not simply in terms of examination passing, but in terms of the quality of the education which had been received and its suitability for the type of students concerned. Some of them, after all, manifestly belong to the world of 'pop' rather than higher culture. It is indeed astonishing how little attention we pay to the end product in our educational system; yet my graduates, like Mr Marris's students, tell some disturbing stories about student philistinism, staff preoccupation and examination cramming which would suggest that, for too many, the process of acquiring a degree is far from being educative. For the good student, the facilities are undoubtedly there; *he* can make very much what he wants of his term of residence. But, for the culturally undernourished, a greater degree of pastoral care, such as is found in training colleges, is needed, a degree of care which it is not perhaps reasonable to expect university teachers, with their vital research commitment to undertake.

But, of course, to conduct such a survey properly, the members of the Robbins committee would have had to have some conception in their minds of what constitutes an educated man; and this is a matter which they—like the society to which they belong—have consistently funked. There is a widely diffused belief throughout our society that somehow, something called education is a good thing: but why it is a good thing— except in so far as it helps to boost production—no one seems quite to know.

And yet, surely an essential element in any claim to be considered educated involves the capacity to be, *in some degree*, detached from the pressure of the immediate. I emphasize 'in some degree' because what I have in mind implies a peculiar combination of detachment and commitment; the detachment must never degenerate into indifference, nor must the commitment blind to the subtle prevarications and falsifications of the over-involved self. We must learn, as Eliot put it, 'to care and not to care'; we must acquire some measure of what he termed 'impersonality', of what Keats called 'negative capability', of what Professor Hofstadter has recently referred to as a combination of 'playfulness' and 'piety'.[1] Only in this way can we see our problems apart from the immediate pressures of our desires and

[1] In *Anti-Intellectualism in American Life.*

184

anxieties and thus have some possibility of seeing them as they truly are. Then the grammar school boy that I referred to earlier will be both rooted and free.

And this, it seems to me, should constitute an essential element in the highest intellectual education the nation provides, that given in universities. The university has a corporate identity transcending immediate political and social exigencies. It is in a unique position to teach its students to realize the permanence which underlies change, the element of repetition in what appears novel, and hence to acquire a certain quality of disinterestedness. Paradoxically, it is by doing this that the university will best serve the community in which it stands, and the culture of which it is a vital part. After all, it is Plato who is still read today, not the Sophists.

II: THE UNIVERSITIES AND BUSINESS

In a recent lecture Sir Paul Chambers, Chairman of ICI, gave it as his opinion that

> In addition to academic education there is a need for the development of certain qualities of character. Life at a University, with its intellectual and inconclusive discussions at postgraduate level is, on the whole, a bad training for the real world; and only men of very strong character surmount this handicap.

Sir Paul voices a feeling about the universities which is quite widespread in industry, though it is not usually formulated so forcefully. What he says, too, given the assumptions in terms of which he is working, is by no means untrue. Though his conception of the university trained mind perhaps owes something to the stereotype of the absent-minded professor (how many graduates has Sir Paul studied?) the general picture of intellectual inconclusiveness which results from a university training bears considerable relationship to a state of mind which, in some contexts at least, is induced by academic study.

I don't know what, precisely, lies behind Sir Pauls' outburst; but it is at least possible that his remarks constitute an indirect way of seeking to gain more influence over university affairs—and, indeed, there are signs of a growing rapprochement between business and the universities. In some respects this is nothing new; for a long time the technological departments of universities have undertaken research which has been useful to industry. But, more recently, it is obvious that, for instance, the Robbins Report has been largely conceived as a response to the need for economic expansion—this, in the terms of that report, is what has constituted the most pressing 'national need'. The Vice-Chancellor of a new university has spoken of seeking to produce the 'all-round graduate of the sort that industry requires'; and the Reith Lectures have revealed how another new university is to be geared, in part, to the requirements of local firms. There is talk of the need for business schools . . . and so on.

The questions therefore arise as to the extent to which industry and business can legitimately make demands on the universities and in what ways. It can be plausibly argued that business constitutes an extremely important part of the social and economic life of the country; that, in the past, universities have not shrunk from vocational training relevant to the professions—among the first university schools were those of medicine and law: why, then, now, should they be queasy about that characteristic twentieth-century vocation—business? Furthermore, the earnings of industry directly or indirectly go to the support of the universities, and should not he who pays the piper call the tune? More insidiously, it is argued that a willingness to cater for the demands of industry will bring tangible rewards in the shape of large gifts—very acceptable for purposes of research, the endowment of chairs, or the erection of imposing new buildings (sometimes, out of deference to the new masters, referred to as 'plant').

And, in fact, for some time now, the educational system has responded at various levels to the growing demands of business. 'The vocational impulse', for example, as the Scottish Brunton Report calls it, is being increasingly appealed to in a variety of

Culture and the University

ways; it is thought to provide motivation for learning as well as to aid economic expansion and to provide a new technical flexibility in line with current educational theories advocating adaptability in the face of the pressures of rapidly changing social circumstances. Furthermore, in the United States, the relationship between business and education has long been close, both at school and at university level. And here, indeed, is something which ought to impel us to press our question about the relationship between business and the universities very forcefully. For, to some of the acutest critics, the American experience has been, in many respects, unfortunate; and, if we are capable of learning from the experience of others—though the record of history is not propitious in this respect—then there is a good deal in current trends which needs to be closely examined.

The major protest against the spread of the business influence in the universities in America was that of Thorstein Veblen in *The Higher Learning in America*. This was first published as long ago as 1918 and was actually mostly written during the nineteen hundreds. The book studied the effects of the growing business interests on the nature of the higher learning and on the recruitment of university presidents and their staffs. Veblen showed that, in general, the universities were being perverted from their high aims of disinterested intellectual enterprise and endeavour by the growing influence of the criteria of practicality and instrumentality on what was studied; and university teachers were themselves being drawn aside from their true vocation as scholars and teachers by the introduction of that spirit of emulation, those values of the market-place, which the gradual assimilation of the business ethos into universities had caused. In view of Sir Paul's outburst, it is relevant to quote from this book published nearly fifty years ago a similar remark:

> More than one of the greater businessmen have spoken advisedly and with emphasis, to the effect that the higher learning is rather a hindrance than a help to any aspirant to business success...

Culture and the University

> If the higher learning is incompatible with business shrewdness,
> business enterprise is, by the same token, incompatible with the
> spirit of the higher learning.

A more recent warning of the dangers to education implicit in
the spread of a business-industrial ideology is to be found in
Professor Callahan's *Education and the Cult of Efficiency*. Here is
chronicled the triumph of 'practicability' and the consequent
impoverishment of the American intellect; here we find how
methods of business efficiency pervaded the public schools and
how, as a result, American educators found themselves de-
graded to the rôle of narrow technicians dedicated to turning
out children in school 'factories' to the 'specifications' laid down
by a business civilization. The book should become required
reading for all who are concerned with education at this particular juncture of our history. Professor Callahan deals with the
schools rather than the universities; but the same ethos affected
the higher learning during the period he covers, as is plain, for
instance, from the protests of the former President of Chicago
University, Robert M. Hutchins.

Why, then, should the universities resist the encroachments of
business? It has been admitted that business is an extremely
important aspect of our social life; the study of society, through
the disciplines of politics, economics, sociology and social
psychology, forms a perfectly legitimate field of university study;
there is, therefore, surely no reason why business should not
form an important element in university study, for facets of
business and industrial life are certainly relevant to the accepted
university disciplines mentioned above.

In these terms business certainly has a legitimate place in the
university. What is important then is that we should always be
quite clear in our minds precisely what these terms are. The job
of a university is to promote understanding; its primary purpose
is the pursuit of truth. It is not concerned with temporary
exigency or immediate practicability. The university need not

necessarily eschew the practical once it is appreciated that it is the fundamental conditions in terms of which the practical operates which are in question, not the mere inculcation of some purely local skill. The sociology of business forms a fascinating and perfectly proper study for a university; but this is business regarded impartially, studied as a facet of a wider social situation, business with all its warts showing. It should be borne in mind that some aspects of the business ethos may well clash with the ethos proper to a university. For the purpose of business is with selling and with profits; if the latter can be fostered, the means used may, without rancour, be regarded as equivocal; it is notorious that the advertiser who seems to be indispensable to the proper conduct of business is willing to employ the suggestion of falsehood, if not the suppression of truth. But it is the function of the university to see the advertiser as he really is, to examine his economic rôle, to assess his wiles in relation to the larger needs of society. An advertising man who has taken a university course in, say, sociology, in which the social incidence of business has played a prominent part, *ought* to be unsure of himself.

For, of course, Sir Paul is right: the effect of a university education ought to be to call into question the whole nature of business. This is not to assert that business has no legitimate rôle to play; but it is one which should see its general function in terms of a larger and more comprehensive social picture. Business provides many services; and it is a poor form of snobbery which makes extensive use of these services—and we all do, today—and, at the same time, considers its processes too contaminated to warrant serious consideration. Nevertheless, its function is essentially that of a provider of means; the goods and services it offers are normally there to serve purposes beyond themselves; their contribution to the good life is essentially subordinate, and in the last resort we could do without many of them, as great civilizations in the past have arisen and flourished without them. To make such essentially mediate functions into important ends is to distort the true function that they can perform and thus to pervert the whole atmosphere of our social life. Fundamentally, it is a trivialising process, one to which we all too easily succumb, but one which should be withstood by one of the few institutions which is still capable of withstanding powerful social pressures, the university.

It is, indeed, the very soul and purpose of the university to encourage that uncertainty of intellectual debate which Sir Paul most criticises—not in order to perplex or obfuscate for its own sake, but because the life of many situations is inherently complex and it is part of their total truth that this should be revealed. Sir Paul finds graduates poor at making decisions; but there is no virtue in making decisions as such—they must be the right decisions. After all, Sir Paul's own decisions about Courtaulds left much to be desired in effectiveness. In any case, efficiency is sometimes at odds with humanity; by 'right decision' I mean to imply something beyond a narrow effectiveness.

But that is not the main point. The main point is that 'intellectual and inconclusive discussions' are the very life-blood of the university. They are, in fact, a very good preparation for real life because in real life there are many topics on which we can only come to tentative conclusions or where a suspended judgment is all that the evidence allows us to make. I suspect that my 'real life' is a rather different one from that which Sir Paul envisages; and this may be a pointer to my fundamental reasons for being chary about allowing business too much say in the affairs of the university. I don't recognize the 'real life' implicit in the businessman's concern as anything more than partial and, to some extent, even dispensable; and I think that the values for which the university should stand, and, if Sir Paul's indictment is correct, obviously does stand, the more vital and sustaining for the modern world.

III: STUDENT CULTURE:

Of cinema attendance at Oxford, Roger Dataller, writing in the early nineteen thirties, had this to say:

Does Hollywood languish unavailingly before the massed allure

Culture and the University

of Theology, Law, Medicine, Literae Humaniores, Modern History, English Language and Literature, Medieval, Modern and Oriental Languages, Physical and Biological Sciences, Philosophy, Politics, and Economics; the Parks, the Union, the Isis and the 'George'? Hollywood does not (*A Pitman Looks at Oxford*).

Exposure of the highly articulate and sophisticated minority thought fit for a university education to mass cultural values is no new phenomenon, then. And, indeed, one would expect the modern Redbrick student to have been subjected to a constant flow of tawdry mass media material which is likely to have formed part of the pattern of his daily living since early childhood. Such material will have nothing like the effect on him that his real intimate family relationships will have had; but, by presenting him with various lying images of reality and encouraging a dispersal of emotional resources through the stimulus to fantasy living afforded, it will have done nothing to help him to grow up—to define the harm in minimal terms.

Furthermore, formal education will largely have ignored the situation. It so happens that in the School of Education at Leicester University I have, for several years, given a number of small volunteer groups of students reading for their post-graduate certificates in education a course on popular culture. I have done the same course with practising teachers reading for an advanced diploma in education, though, here, I shall draw more on my experience with the former group. My work with these different groups of students has led me to see how isolated from their everyday interests and attachments their specifically academic concerns are for many of them. The words 'artificial' and 'alien' crop up frequently in students' discussions of their experience of university life—as Mr. Peter Marris, for instance, bears out in his recently published *The Experience of Higher Education*, and as I have certainly noticed among my own students. One comes to see why. Often, university disciplines are not seen as means to clarification of the world in various of its more sophisticated guises, as means, that is, to *understanding*, but as bodies of knowledge to be learnt for the purpose of getting a degree. These bodies of knowledge themselves vary in their closeness to, or distance from, the major preoccupations of late adolescence—literature, history, the social sciences, for instance, can have considerable immediate relevance to problems of sex and relationship which are of great significance to young people of student age, though even these subjects are not always seen in this way. (The idea that a discipline might have importance and significance precisely because it does *not* bear on immediate interests but permits an extension of consciousness in realms beyond the reach of 'practicality' is a notion too remote and sophisticated for our pragmatic age.) Even when university disciplines are directed specifically at the world, as most of those studied at Redbrick are, by implication, today, it is still hard for the average student to make much real connection between his subject and life as he knows it—other than in terms of a degree and the expectation of a job. And the idea that vocation itself is something which should spill over into general living, instead of being merely an element in the work-leisure dichotomy, is foreign to many of those even who are training to be teachers.

It is because the academic often seems 'alien' and 'artificial', then, that many students fail to appreciate some of the real problems of mass culture. In my seminars, most of the students reveal themselves as deeply knowledgeable of TV and 'pop' idol folklore; they will often debate, at some length, the relative merits of the different TV serial regulars and of the pop groups. In general, by comparison with those of the populace at large, their comments are fairly sophisticated, at least in the sense that they are often highly critical. Even so, they can reveal some remarkably naïve acceptances; and, when they reject (as they do with advertisements, for instance) they often do so out of a comprehensive, all-pervading cynicism that reminds me forcibly of the feeling I remember so well from my own undergraduate days in the 'thirties, that of believing everything to be a 'racket'; it was a feeling summed up for my generation by the Journalist's song and chorus in W. H. Auden's *Dog Beneath the Skin*: 'They're in the racket, too'. Of course, it tends to be the more politically

Culture and the University

conscious students who take this line, as in the 'thirties—like the bright, articulate young man who suddenly, startlingly, and rather irrelevantly, introduced a reference to that 'Bitch at Buckingham Palace' and took me back to the time when most of my clever contemporaries read the *Daily Worker* and accepted its grotesque parody of capitalist society, of which the monarchy was a part. It's called being anti-Establishment, today.

In general, these post-graduate groups hover between acceptance and rejection in terms which suggest that the attitudes constitute two sides of the same coin. The world of popular culture is too much a part of their world, enters too deeply into their consciousness for them to be able to regard it with any real degree of emotional detachment. Those who accept it, see it as 'entertainment', 'relaxation' or say 'you can't work all the time', 'it takes you out of yourself', 'everybody has a right to his own taste' or 'taste is relative'—providing stepping stones to the haven of justification. Those who reject are either those who do so on political grounds, as I have noted above (and their rejection tends to be partial because they accept the culture of 'pop' protest, like that of TW3 with its combination of cynicism and sentimentality) or those who have received a literary training and have duly read their *Culture and Environment* and the other writings associated with it. Sometimes I fear that some of these latter have learnt their lesson with the more conscious parts of their personalities; they project horror and disgust, but one feels that occasionally they are secretly attracted. What practically none of them is capable of is seeing why, and in what terms, most of popular culture appeals. They fail to see that most of it arises out of a deficiency in emotional vitality; it appeals to thwarted desires raised to a higher pitch of expectation than ever before by the accomplishments of applied science and yet faced by the emotionally desiccated universe that science has left us with. They do not realize that much of this culture represents a degradation from what, in times past, the ordinary folk have been able to achieve because, of course, they are profoundly ignorant of the cultural history of their own society and of the very real accomplishments of the folk of the past. School education has replaced the traditional folk consciousness, and it would be a bold man who urged that the change had always been for the better; sensibilities are too often adrift on the scraps and orts of 'knowledge' ('knowledge' without understanding) which their schooling has provided them with. Many of the students' families, too, in the post-industrial era, have lost touch; it is not surprising that so many are so emotionally immature. Even their criticisms tend to be criticisms within the terms implied by pop culture; they lack the perspectives which would enable them to judge it by an older tradition or to see it as one response (Hitler was another) to an emotionally impoverished era, as a sort of decadent romanticism.

It is this which explains, partly, their 'alienation' from the university. Paradoxically, the university, far from being 'artificial', represents 'reality' in a variety of highly sophisticated, consciously articulated guises. Yet to a fair proportion of undergraduates it doesn't appear this way. This is partly because many of them enter what might be termed a 'pop' university, a place which has been imaged in press and popular novel and where revelation is simply waiting round the corner. The disappointment some students feel with their university careers arises out of the impossible demands they have initially made on the university: they have arrived with no appreciation of the gradualness of understanding and of the conditions of slow accretion under which alone such understanding can be arrived at. The pop world is one of quick and easy returns; knowledge is a matter of facts remembered for regurgitation at quizzes. 'The Brain of Britain' is he who can remember unlikely and irrelevant pieces of information. Such notions and values conflict with what the university has to offer. It is not surprising that 'knowledge' as understanding escapes many of them.

They are not always helped as much as they might be by their mentors. The tastes and acceptances of university dons are themselves worthy of study; they, too, are often more seduced by 'entertainment' values than one might imagine—conversation over lunch reveals some unsuspected allegiances to very inferior soap opera material. This is part of the penalty of

Culture and the University

increased professionalization and the consequent narrowing of expertise—an unavoidable concomitant of the current explosion of knowledge.

The world of 'pop' is a pervasive presence in the university. In response, we need two things—an assertion of the *reality* of the university and a discrimination within the world of 'pop' itself which sees it as part of the developed consciousness of the folk under industrial and commercial conditions. Not all 'pop' is entirely bad—though most of it is appalling—but it needs to be judged in relation to the best folk art of the past.

Index

Index

Index

Index

Index

Index